Other Poetry Anthologies
Compiled by
Vardell and Wong

The Poetry Friday Anthology
K–5 Editions

Poems for the School Year
with Connections to the Common Core
K–5 Edition

Poems for the School Year
with Connections to the TEKS
K–5 Edition

The PoetryTagTime Trio
the first-ever electronic anthologies
of original poetry
for children and teens

PoetryTagTime
30 Poets - Poems for K–5

P*TAG
31 Poets - Poems for Teens

Gift Tag
Holiday Poems for K–8

The Poetry Friday Anthology
for Middle School

Poems for the School Year
with Connections to the TEKS

Middle School Edition
Grades 6–8

110 poems by 71 poets

compiled by
Sylvia Vardell and Janet Wong

pomelo ∗ books

✳ ✳ ✳

this book is dedicated to
all the poets
in our anthologies
for their generosity and inspiration

No part of this publication may be reproduced, or stored in a retrieval system, or transmitted in any form or by any means, electronic, mechanical, photocopying, recording, or otherwise, without written permission of the publisher. For information regarding permission, please contact us:

Pomelo Books
4580 Province Line Road
Princeton, NJ 08540
www.PomeloBooks.com
info@PomeloBooks.com

Text/compilation copyright ©2013 by Sylvia M. Vardell and Janet S. Wong.
All rights reserved.

Individual poems copyright ©2013 by the individual poets. All rights reserved.

Library of Congress Cataloging-in-Publication Data is available.

ISBN 978-1-937057-87-9

Please visit us:
www.PomeloBooks.com

Poems By

Joy Acey	Renée M. LaTulippe
Jeannine Atkins	Gail Carson Levine
Carmen T. Bernier-Grand	Debbie Levy
Robyn Hood Black	J. Patrick Lewis
Calef Brown	George Ella Lyon
Joseph Bruchac	Guadalupe Garcia McCall
Jen Bryant	Heidi Mordhorst
Leslie Bulion	Marilyn Nelson
Stephanie Calmenson	Lesléa Newman
Deborah Chandra	Naomi Shihab Nye
Kate Coombs	Ann Whitford Paul
Cynthia Cotten	Jack Prelutsky
Kristy Dempsey	Mary Quattlebaum
Margarita Engle	Heidi Bee Roemer
Betsy Franco	Michael J. Rosen
Carole Gerber	Deborah Ruddell
Charles Ghigna	Laura Purdie Salas
Joan Bransfield Graham	Michael Salinger
Nikki Grimes	Ted Scheu
Lorie Ann Grover	Joyce Sidman
Monica Gunning	Marilyn Singer
Mary Lee Hahn	Ken Slesarik
Avis Harley	Sonya Sones
David L. Harrison	Eileen Spinelli
Terry Webb Harshman	Holly Thompson
Juanita Havill	Amy Ludwig VanDerwater
Georgia Heard	Lee Wardlaw
Stephanie Hemphill	Charles Waters
Sara Holbrook	April Halprin Wayland
Carol-Ann Hoyte	Robert Weinstock
Patricia Hubbell	Steven Withrow
Jacqueline Jules	Allan Wolf
X.J. Kennedy	Virginia Euwer Wolff
Linda Kulp	Janet Wong
Julie Larios	Jane Yolen
Irene Latham	

*"When power corrupts, **poetry cleanses**. For art establishes the basic human truth which must serve as the touchstone of our judgment."*

— John F. Kennedy

Table of Contents

What Is Poetry Friday?	8
Poetry and the TEKS	11
Why Poetry?	13
Poetry Breaks	14
Read-Aloud Strategies	15
How to Use the *Take 5!* Box	16
Lexiles and Levels	18
Which Poems Should We Read?	19
A Poem for Everyone: "First Day at a New School"	23
Poetry TEKS for Sixth Grade	26
Poems for Sixth Grade	27
Poetry TEKS for Seventh Grade	102
Poems for Seventh Grade	103
Poetry TEKS for Eighth Grade	178
Poems for Eighth Grade	179
A Poem for Everyone: "The Last Day of School"	253
Building Your Own Poetry Library	256
Poetry Websites and Blogs	257
E-Resources for Poetry Teaching	259
Professional Resource Books	260
A Mini-Glossary of Poetry Terms	261
About the Poets	262
Copyright and Permissions	264
Title Index	265
Poet Index	267
Poem Credits	269
TGIF!	276
Acknowledgments	279
About Sylvia Vardell	280
About Janet Wong	281

What Is Poetry Friday?

In 2006 blogger Kelly Herold brought Poetry Friday to the "kidlitosphere." Much like "casual Friday" in the corporate world, there is a perception in the world of literature that on Fridays we should relax a bit and take a moment for something special.

Why not bring the Poetry Friday concept into your classroom, taking five minutes every Friday to share a poem and explore it a bit, connect it with children's lives, and capitalize on a teachable moment? Pausing to share a poem—and reinforce a language skill—on Poetry Friday is an easy way to infuse poetry into your current teaching practice.

On Poetry Friday you can find blog posts that include original poems, book reviews, song lyrics, poetry curriculum tips, and more. Each Friday a different blogger volunteers to gather and host a list of poetry posts from participating blogs. For a list of participating bloggers, see *25 Poetry Websites and Blogs You Need to Know* on page 258.

Yes, of course you can share poetry on other days of the week too—and we hope that you will! But for those who are not already teaching poetry regularly, planning for Poetry Friday makes poetry sharing intentional rather than incidental. **And once you have celebrated a month of Poetry Fridays, we promise that students will be clamoring for it.**

Poetry and the TEKS

"**Poetry** is not only dream and vision; it is the skeleton architecture of our lives. It **lays the foundations for a future of change**, a bridge across our fears of what has never been before."

⁂ Audre Lorde ⁂

Poetry and the TEKS

The state-adopted curriculum provides a framework that informs all instruction in Texas. These Texas Essential Knowledge and Skills (TEKS) also include a component focused on teaching students about poetry. That provides a central focus for this book. This book is first and foremost a quality anthology of original poetry for young people written by 71 of today's most popular poets. Students in any state (or country) can enjoy, explore, and respond to these poems. However, we have also come to realize that educators, librarians, and parents are looking for guidance in how to share poetry with young people and teach the skills within the curriculum as well. Thus, this book offers both: quality poetry plus curriculum-based suggestions for helping students enjoy and understand poetry more deeply.

What are the expectations outlined in the TEKS?

In **grade six,** we focus on helping students understand the structure and elements of poetry, how figurative language contributes to meaning, and how a poet uses sensory language to create imagery. We guide them in making inferences and drawing conclusions and challenge them to support their opinions with examples from the poem. We can help them understand how poets create meaning through figurative language and stylistic elements, including alliteration, onomatopoeia, personification, metaphors, similes, and hyperbole, as well as the use of graphic elements like refrains, line length, and line breaks.

In **grade seven,** we continue our focus on helping students understand the structure and elements of poetry, challenging them to make inferences and draw conclusions supported by evidence from the poem. In addition, we guide them in seeing how figurative language (such as personification, idioms, and hyperbole) contributes to meaning and how a poet uses sensory language to create imagery. We help them determine the figurative meaning of phrases and how the poet uses language to suggest mood. We also consider the importance of graphic elements (e.g., capital letters, line length, word position) on the meaning of a poem and how poets use rhyme scheme and meter in distinctive ways.

Our ongoing focus on helping students understand the structure and elements of poetry continues in **grade eight**, along with the expectation that students can provide support for their inferences and conclusions drawn from the poems themselves. We continue to guide them in understanding how a poet's use of sensory language creates imagery in poetry and how figurative language such as personification, idioms, and hyperbole contributes to a poem's meaning. In addition, we can explore the effects of similes and extended metaphors in more complex poetry. We also consider the importance of graphic elements (e.g., word position) on the meaning of a poem and how poets use rhyme scheme and meter in distinctive ways. Finally, we now challenge students to compare and contrast the relationship between the purpose and characteristics of different poetic forms (e.g., epic poetry, lyric poetry).

The keys to remember are:

- A poem should first be enjoyed for its own sake.
- Presenting poems in participatory ways (in various choral strategies) gets your learner "into the poem."
- The main idea is to help your learner see and hear the poetic elements after enjoying the poem through multiple readings—and to come through the "back door" to skills.

Reading Poetry Aloud

A guiding principle of this book is that **poetry is meant to be read aloud**. As the award-winning poet Eve Merriam noted, "It's easier to savor the flavor of the words as they roll around in your mouth for your ears to enjoy." Like song lyrics that sit quietly on the page, the music of poetry comes alive when spoken and shared. It is also the ideal way to approach poetry instruction.

The more students hear, read, say, and experience the poem, the more they internalize the sounds, words, and meanings of the poem and begin to notice the mechanics and artistry of poetry.

Here are some tips to help you read aloud effectively:

- Be sure to *say the title and author* of the poem.
- If possible, *display the words of the poem* while you read it aloud.
- Be sure to *enunciate each word* distinctly (and check uncertain pronunciations beforehand).
- *Glance at the audience* occasionally.
- *Add to the effect with a portable microphone*, using a microphone app.

Why Poetry?

When we think about what poetry does for young people—and in just a few minutes of sharing on a regular basis—it's a pretty impressive list. Educators David Booth and Bill Moore note, "Like film makers or photographers, poets manipulate our ears and eyes at the same time, using close-ups, long shots, slow motion, fast-forward, and soft focus; they juxtapose sound and image to make new meanings; they weave in subplots and overlap scenes; and they do it at lightning speed, in a few lines, in one word." Here are some key benefits to sharing poetry with young people:

- Poetry reinforces word sounds, rimes, rhymes, patterns, and pronunciation.

- Poetry introduces new vocabulary and figurative language, as well as examples of synonyms, antonyms, puns, word play, and coining of new words and expressions.

- Poetry is rich in imagery that stimulates the imagination.

- Poetry often includes sensory language that communicates the senses of sight, smell, touch, and hearing.

- Poetry offers an emotional connection and can reflect and elicit powerful and deeply felt moments.

- Poetry provides practice for oral language development, listening, and oral fluency, as well as a bridge to understanding the written word.

- Poetry has pedagogical uses across the curriculum (e.g., building science concepts, reinforcing historical themes, adding motivation to math lessons), making it an effective tool for connecting with nonfiction.

- Poetry can heighten awareness of the use of mechanical conventions, from spacing and margins to commas and quotation marks.

- Poetry is accessible to a wide range of reading abilities and language learning skill levels.

- Poetry has a long shelf life and poems can be revisited again and again, prompting different responses at different ages and stages.

Poetry Breaks

Whether you introduce a poem at the beginning of the day, when transitioning to lunch, during a break, or when wrapping things up, "breaking" for poetry provides a moment to refresh and engage. Of course, this doesn't mean that a more in-depth study of poetry is not a good idea. It is. But for the average teacher or librarian, consistently sharing a five-minute poem break is an effective practice. Communicate to students that a poetry break is about to begin by using a sign, bell, signal, or chime announcing "Poetry Break!"

Our Take 5 activities rely heavily on reading the poem aloud—and in multiple ways—as well as talking about the poem and following up with more oral reading of more poetry. We also provide specific guidelines for how to approach each poem in creative ways. Here are a few guidelines from *Poetry Everywhere* by Jack Collom and Sheryl Noethe.

- Be yourself. You needn't and shouldn't show reverence for poetry by means of an artificially dignified atmosphere.
- Energy is the key—but it shouldn't be forced. A brisk pace is good, as long as you slow down when the situation needs it.
- Practice reading with pauses at ends of lines and in other places; think about how this affects the understanding of a poem.
- It's helpful to admit your own errors and ignorance. Poetry can be ambiguous and poetry rules are sometimes unclear.
- Decide what you're going to do and go for it. Relax. Concentrate. Freely intersperse humor and seriousness. Have fun!

---

3 Fun and Easy Ways to Celebrate Poetry

"Poetry Celebrations" give your students something to look forward to and can provide opportunities for engagement. For more ideas, consult *The Poetry Teacher's Book of Lists* by Sylvia Vardell.

1. If audio announcements are made on a regular basis, encourage students to volunteer for a performance reading of a favorite poem with sound effects or musical instruments.

2. Invite students to perform their own poem readings on the last Friday of the month (or other set day) as a Poetry Friday event. Create a coffee house setting with tablecloths, bongos, and a microphone for fun. Record some of the readings for a school or local cable television program.

3. Partner with an elementary school classroom, senior center, hospital, or local business to share favorite poems selected by or original poems written by the students. Create simple poetry posters, booklets, or mini-movies featuring poems to share with an outside audience.

Read-Aloud Strategies

For each poem, we provide suggestions for how to invite students to participate in reading the poem aloud. Often the poem itself will "show" you how to perform it if you study the lines and their arrangement on the page. And when you invite students to participate in poem performance, you will find that they will have ideas about how to try a poem this way or that way. Follow their lead! It is also good to remember that, in the middle school years as they move from leaving elementary school to preparing for high school, students evolve quite a bit between grades. Vocal, whole-class strategies will be more effective and popular in grade six, but by grade eight, students may prefer more peer-centric activities with a partner or small group. Here are some general guidelines for involving middle school students in reading poetry out loud.

- **Take the lead,** be the first to read the poem, and don't be afraid to "ham it up." Take the pressure off students by showing how the poem sounds, how words should be pronounced, how the meaning and emotion might be conveyed. Don't ask them to do anything you wouldn't do yourself.

- **Use props** whenever possible to make a concrete connection to the poem, focus attention, and add a bit of fun. Choose something suggested by the poem. It's even worth planning ahead to have a good prop ready beforehand. Students can then use the props too as they volunteer to join in on reading the poem, taking the focus off of them and giving the audience something specific to look at while listening—the poetry prop.

- **Try using media** to add another dimension to the poetry experience. Look for digital images or videos relevant to the poem to display without sound as a backdrop while reading the poem aloud, or find music or sound effects suggested by the poem to underscore the meaning or mood as you read the poem aloud.

- **Offer choices** as you invite students to join in on reading the poem aloud with you. They can choose a favorite line to chime in on or volunteer to read a line or stanza of their choice or ask a friend to join them in reading a portion aloud. The more say they have about how they participate in the poem reading, the more eager and comfortable they will be about volunteering.

- **Make connections** between the poems and their lives and experiences, between one poem and another, and between poems and other genres like nonfiction, short stories, newspaper articles, and songs). We provide example questions and poem connections for each poem, but once you have established that pattern, be open to the connections the students themselves make first.

- **Be creative** and use art, drama, and technology to present the poem and to engage students in participating in that presentation. Find relevant photos, draw quick Pictionary-style sketches, make word clouds, create graphic "novel" comic panels for poem lines, use American Sign Language for key words, pose in a dramatic "frozen" tableau, collaborate on a PowerPoint slide show, and so on. Look to share the poem in a way that is particularly meaningful for middle school students. Or better yet, let them show you!

How to Use the *Take 5!* Box

Each poem in this book faces a *Take 5!* box of teaching tips. Below you will find the *Take 5!* box for the opening poem, "First Day at a New School" by Julie Larios (A Poem for Everyone, page 23).

Take 5!

1. **Display a photo or website image of the school** or, if possible, a map of the school, while reading this poem aloud.

2. With 22 lines, **this poem is ideal for 22 volunteers to take one line each to read aloud** along with you. Read the poem aloud again and invite volunteers to join in on individual lines of their choice. Alert them to the poet's use of question marks for intonation cues. Try it faster and faster to convey the breathless anxiety—and relief—in the poem.

3. For discussion: *Which worries could we add to this poem?*

4. Poets arrange their words quite purposefully to create a certain effect. Discuss with students how this poem might look and feel if it were one continuous prose paragraph. Here, **the poet uses one- and two-word phrases and questions in a list format** to give the poem a distinctive rhythm and tone.

5. Compare this poem with a slightly different take on the same subject, **"First Week of School" by Janet Wong** (6th Grade, Week 1, page 29).

While the content for each *Take 5!* box is tailored to the individual poems, all *Take 5!* boxes contain the same sequence of teaching tips for consistency and ease of use. Again, these are only suggested activities and curriculum connections. You'll want to pick and choose which suggestions work best for your students.

Tip #1: This first tip provides an easy suggestion for how to make the poem come alive as you read it aloud by pairing the poem with a prop, adding gestures or movement, trying out specific dramatic reading techniques, adding multi-media, and so on.

Tip #2: This tip suggests how to engage students in participating with you in reading the poem aloud. For example, look for any repeated words, phrases, lines, or stanzas in the poem. Highlight or display the words, inviting students to chime in on only those words as you read the rest of the poem aloud.

Tip #3: You'll find a fun discussion prompt here, tailored to fit the poem. It's usually an open-ended question with no single, correct answer. Encourage diversity in responses!

Tip #4: We designed this tip to connect the poem to a specific language arts or poetry skill or concept such as rhyme, repetition, alliteration, and onomatopoeia. Also, this is where we point out poetic forms and structures, as well as explain techniques such as personification and simile.

Tip #5: In this tip we share related poem titles and poetry book titles that connect well with the featured poem based on poet, subject, form, or use of poetic devices. You can find additional poetry connections and cross-genre connections at the **Poetry Friday Anthology blog,** the **PFAMS blog,** and the **Poetry for Children blog**. See the list *25 Poetry Websites and Blogs You Need to Know* on page 258 for these and other blog addresses.

Weekly Themes

Share a poem every Friday, and over the course of the school year you will have introduced 36 different original poems by contemporary poets on some of the most popular themes and topics in poetry for young people.

Each week has a designated theme that crosses all levels, 6–8. This provides a school-wide connection as each grade enjoys a different poem on the same topic.

Themes and topics begin with school itself and also include fun and games, pets, weather, food, families, communities, holidays, the human body, art, friendship, kindness, science and technology, music and dance, summer vacation, and rhythm, rhyme, repetition, metaphor, simile, and personification.

You will find multiple connections across the curriculum (in science, history, art, and music) with endless possibilities for collaboration and expansion.

Lexiles and Levels

The readability level of poems varies greatly since poetry doesn't easily fit the use of Lexiles and levels. Simple poems can have very sophisticated vocabulary and long poems can use simple language. Determining Lexile levels is based on a variety of factors such as how long the sentences are and how unusual the words are, as well as on the use of basic punctuation. The nursery rhyme "Little Jack Horner," for example, is written at the same eighth grade level as Robert Frost's classic poem "Stopping by Woods on a Snowy Evening." But clearly they are significantly different works. The power lies in a poem's meaning and in the distinctive ways the poet uses and arranges words. With these principles in mind, **this anthology presents poems for each grade level selected for their relevance, interest, and appropriateness for each grade.**

Conclusion

Read these poems aloud so that students of all abilities and language learning levels can participate in the poem. Display the words so that students can have visual as well as aural reinforcement. (One easy way to do this is to project the e-book version of this book from your computer.) Invite students to join in saying words and reading the text as they make the poem their own. Talk about the poems and encourage students to share what they notice, then build on their knowledge to expand that skills base. Link the poems with more poems, more poets, and more poetry books. Infuse poem-sharing throughout the day and throughout the curriculum. Mark this book up with notes about your students' responses to individual poems. **And don't be surprised if it's a wonderful poem moment that students remember most vividly at the end of the school year!**

WHICH POEMS SHOULD WE READ?

We offer a set of 36 poems—a poem-a-week for the 9 months of the typical school year—for each grade level and have designed activities that are poem-specific, skill-based, and developmentally appropriate for each weekly poem.

Our goal is to provide support for educators and parents who might be unfamiliar with today's poetry for young people and might need guidance in how to begin. For each poem you share, we suggest another poem from the book that is related in some way.

Feel free to share any and all of the poems with the students you teach at any time, in any order, and in any way you like.

The Poems

A Poem for Everyone

Take 5!

1. **Display a photo or website image of the school** or, if possible, a map of the school, while reading this poem aloud.

2. With 22 lines, **this poem is ideal for 22 volunteers to take one line each to read aloud** along with you. Read the poem aloud again and invite volunteers to join in on individual lines of their choice. Alert them to the poet's use of question marks for intonation cues. Try it faster and faster to convey the breathless anxiety—and relief—in the poem.

3. For discussion: *Which worries could we add to this poem?*

4. Poets arrange their words quite purposefully to create a certain effect. Discuss with students how this poem might look and feel if it were one continuous prose paragraph. Here, **the poet uses one and two-word phrases and questions in a list format** to give the poem a distinctive rhythm and tone.

5. Compare this poem with a slightly different take on the same subject, **"First Week of School" by Janet Wong** (6th Grade, Week 1, page 29).

First Day at a New School
by Julie Larios

Big place! Middle school.
Settle down. Deep breath.
Okay. Here goes.
Oh-oh. Schedule?
Locker? Homeroom?
B-Wing? French class?
Which desk? Bonjour?
Bell again? Staircase?
Science lab? Math?
History? Hungry?
Lunch room? Which table?
Food's good—and friends!
Bell again? So quick?
A-Wing? Which way?
Bell again? Library?
Checkout? Which way?
PE? Gym?
Teammates? Final bell?
Combination? Homework?
Books? Backpack?
Which bus? Which seat?
My stop? Whew!

*"Poetry is the journal of a sea animal living on land, **wanting to fly in the air**."*

☙ Carl Sandburg ❧

Poems for Sixth Grade

Poetry TEKS for Sixth Grade
(110.18. (b) (4); (8); (15 B i, ii, iii))

In **grade six,** we focus on helping students understand:

- the structure and elements of poetry
- how figurative language contributes to meaning
- how a poet uses sensory language to create imagery
- making inferences and drawing conclusions about poems
- supporting opinions with examples from the poem
- how poets create meaning through figurative language
- stylistic elements and figurative language including alliteration, onomatopoeia, personification, metaphors, similes, and hyperbole
- the use of refrains, line length, and line breaks

Sixth Grade

week 1	School	First Week of School *by Janet Wong*
week 2	More School	Locker Ness Monster *by Robyn Hood Black*
week 3	Fun & Games	Tryouts *by Jen Bryant*
week 4	Pets	Cat Hockey *by Lee Wardlaw*
week 5	More Pets	He Was So Little *by David L. Harrison*
week 6	On the Ground	Consider the Bombardier Beetle *by Jane Yolen*
week 7	In the Water	Dear Monster of Loch Ness *by Jack Prelutsky*
week 8	In the Air	Night Light *by Carole Gerber*
week 9	Weather	Racing the Clouds *by Jacqueline Jules*
week 10	Food	Names *by Julie Larios*
week 11	More Food	Food One-Worders *by J. Patrick Lewis*
week 12	House & Home	The Waking House *by Charles Ghigna*
week 13	Families	Mom Talk *by Kristy Dempsey*
week 14	Community	First Practice *by Amy Ludwig VanDerwater*
week 15	Stuff We Love	Giving *by Jane Yolen*
week 16	Holidays	Wong's Café *by Janet Wong*
week 17	Time Together	Fishing Trip *by Charles Waters*
week 18	Human Body	Your Appendix Is a Mystery *by Allan Wolf*
week 19	More Human Body	A Light Reaction *by Carol-Ann Hoyte*
week 20	Art & Colors	Sixth Grade Art Class *by Deborah Ruddell*
week 21	Love & Friendship	Advice to Rapunzel *by Eileen Spinelli*
week 22	A Kinder Place	Lost *by Kate Coombs*
week 23	Exploring	Dromedary Ferry *by Juanita Havill*
week 24	Science & Tech	Silence *by Linda Kulp*
week 25	Song & Dance	Opening Night *by Renée M. LaTulippe*
week 26	Nonsense	Mere Shadow *by Robert Weinstock*
week 27	World of Words	Ack! *by Cynthia Cotten*
week 28	Books	Meet The Saurus *by Heidi Mordhorst*
week 29	Poetry Poems	In the Word Woods *by April Halprin Wayland*
week 30	RR&R	Convection *by Joyce Sidman*
week 31	Different Forms	Future Hoopsters *by Avis Harley*
week 32	Metaphor & Simile	That Boat *by George Ella Lyon*
week 33	Personification	Pen *by Nikki Grimes*
week 34	On the Move	Texas, Out Driving *by Naomi Shihab Nye*
week 35	Summer Vacation	Cousins *by Charles Waters*
week 36	Looking Forward	I Know I'm Going Somewhere *by Ted Scheu*

WEEK 1: SCHOOL

Take 5!

1. Before presenting this school-themed poem, **display one or two contrasting school photos of yourself from the past** (e.g., elementary school, middle school, college), if you have them. Or look for vintage photos of students from years gone by on Shorpy.com.

2. Share the poem aloud again, but this time **invite three volunteers to read the lines with observations** about various people. (They can each choose a partner if needed for extra confidence.) One student or pair reads line 4 and line 7; another reads line 5 and line 8; and the third reads line 6 and line 9. You read the first and final stanzas to set the stage and wrap it up.

3. For discussion: *What are the worst and best parts of the first week of school?*

4. Poets arrange their words and lines in a variety of ways to give their poems a certain rhythm and to add to the meaning of the poem. Here, **the poet uses the three-line tercet for each stanza** and repeats the first line of the poem, with a slight variation, in the first line of the final stanza to "frame" the poem. Talk about how the poet uses rhyme to link the lines in each stanza, including end rhyme (*show/know/go; small/tall/hall; show/slow/know*) and "slant" or "almost" rhyme (*thin/him/been*). Then read the poem aloud again.

5. Share another poem with a "new year" theme also written by **Janet Wong**: "Another New Year" (7th Grade, Week 1, page 105).

WEEK 1: SCHOOL

FIRST WEEK OF SCHOOL
by **Janet Wong**

First week here: it's like a show.
Lots of kids that I don't know.
Where am I supposed to go?

Cameron got super-tall and thin.
Sam's working out—look at him!
Hey, Steve! Where have you been?

Is that Caitlyn? Caitlyn's small.
That girl there is definitely tall.
I think my room's at the end of this hall.

First week: wow, what a show!
I'm glad this crowded hall's so slow.
Lots of kids I already know!

WEEK 2: MORE SCHOOL

Take 5!

1. Add a bit of fun to sharing this poem with a "poetry prop"—**hold up a locker lock** before reading the poem aloud. Spin the wheel and stop at the numbers in the poem (24/18/6; 26/14/8; 26/18/4). See if you can do that WHILE reading the poem aloud!

2. In sharing the poem aloud again, **students can randomly join in on saying the number words** in the first, third, and fifth stanzas while you read the whole poem out loud.

3. For discussion: *What is the secret to managing life with lockers?*

4. Repetition is a key ingredient in creating poems. Sometimes a poet uses repetition not just to enhance the sound of the poem, but to emphasize meaning. **Lead the students in discussing how the poet repeats the number words** in this poem in different configurations of similar-sounding numbers to heighten the sense of confusion expressed in the poem.

5. Follow up with another poem involving confusion over numbers: **"Fourths of Me" by Betsy Franco** (7th Grade, Week 30, page 163). If you have the instruction page for a locker lock handy, compare the language in that pamphlet with the language in this poem.

LOCKER NESS MONSTER
by Robyn Hood Black

Twenty-four
Eighteen
Six.

Arrrgh. That's not it.

Twenty-six
Fourteen
Eight.

Nothing. Nada. Nyet.

Twenty-six
Eighteen
Four.

CLICK. **That's it!**

Unlock your head,
then your fingers,
then the door.

WEEK 3: FUN & GAMES

Take 5!

1. Bring a whistle, a soccer ball, or an orange marker cone to use as a prop to set the stage before sharing this poem aloud. Then pause dramatically between the stanzas, **altering your voice slightly for the italicized lines that signal the coach's instructions**.

2. In a follow-up reading, **ask for a student volunteer to say the two indented and italicized stanzas attributed to the coach.** If you're feeling brave, offer the student the use of the whistle prop, too.

3. **Invite students to share two or three stories about favorite coaches** from school or from outside activities.

4. Sometimes poets use basic graphic elements like italics, capital letters, punctuation, spacing, and indentation to add interest to their poems. Guide students in discussing how some of these components in this poem help show us how to read the poem, particularly **the arrangement of stanzas and the representation of the coach's voice with indented and italicized text.**

5. Share another poem about soccer by **Jen Bryant, "World Cup"** (7th Grade, Week 36, page 175), or selections from *And the Crowd Goes Wild!: A Global Gathering of Sports Poems*, edited by Carol-Ann Hoyte and Heidi Bee Roemer. Or for a completely different kind of sports writing, select a recent newspaper article about school sports, particularly soccer, and contrast that writer's approach with Jen Bryant's use of language and arrangement of words in this poem.

TRYOUTS
by Jen Bryant

Thirty-two players
for sixteen spots.
My hands are sweaty,
my stomach's in knots.

See these cones?
Dribble around, then stop.
Pass off to the left,
then take a shot . . .

On your mark, I get set
for the timed shuttle run—
back and forth, back and forth
(listen for the gun).

OK girls, here's what you'll do.
Now count off: One-Two . . .
Face your opponent,
tackle, turn, sprint through.

We line up for long balls,
headers, corner kicks;
the whole time I'm praying
my name will make his list.

WEEK 4: PETS

Take 5!

1. **Bring a broom or hockey stick** and scoot around the room a bit as if you were playing hockey before—or while—reading the poem aloud.

2. **Invite students to chime in on the response word or phrase to each real or implied question** (*the rink; The stick; Lunch!*). Cue them by raising your hockey stick or broom.

3. For discussion: *If cats play hockey, what sport might dogs aspire to play?*

4. Many poems rhyme, but not all. This is an example of a poem form that usually does not rhyme, a haiku poem. **Originally a Japanese form of poetry, a haiku typically focuses on the natural world in only three lines (generally 5 syllables, 7 syllables, 5 syllables).** Guide students in understanding the haiku form with this example.

5. Compare this poem with another haiku, **"Feather" by Marilyn Singer** (7th Grade, Week 6, page 115), or selections from Lee Wardlaw's haiku picture book, *Won Ton*.

CAT HOCKEY
by Lee Wardlaw

Waxed floor: the rink. My
paw? The stick. Tailless lizard
serves as puck. Goal? Lunch!

Sixth Grade

Week 5: More Pets

Take 5!

1. Before **reading this poem (in a quiet voice)**, set the stage by reminding students that many poems are funny, but some are serious—like this one.

2. In a follow-up reading, form six groups of students and **challenge each group to create a quick visual for one stanza of the poem** (six groups, six stanzas—one stanza each). Then read the poem aloud again, showing each visual (e.g., an Internet image or a sketch) for each stanza as you read. Display a copy of the poem alongside a collage of these images.

3. For a cross-genre connection, look for the nonfiction book *ER Vets: Life in an Animal Emergency Room* by Donna Jackson, or research pet first aid on the Internet. **Compare excerpts of factual narrative with this poem in terms of approach, information shared, and emotional impact.**

4. This is an example of a poem that "reads like a video" and is full of description and imagery. Poets often use sensory language to create poem pictures. Talk with students about how key words are used in this poem to paint a picture in your mind, and **challenge them to identify which words and phrases are most vivid and sensory** (*eyes bright; puddles so little; head hanging; ears drooping; loud noises; made him whimper; hold him against my chest; shivering stopped*). After this discussion, share the whole poem aloud again.

5. Compare this with another poem about saying goodbye to a pet: **"Doors of the 24-Hour Emergency Veterinary Hospital" by Virginia Euwer Wolff** (8th Grade, Week 5, page 189).

HE WAS SO LITTLE
by David L. Harrison

Couldn't reach a chair,
just stood there begging,
eyes bright, fanny wagging
until I reached down.

His puddles were so little
sometimes I'd miss them,
but he always gave himself away,
head hanging,
ears drooping,
ashamed.

Loud noises scared him,
made him whimper,
come running to me
too scared to know what to do.
I'd pick him up,
hold him against my chest
till the shivering stopped.

We grew up together
except I got bigger,
he just got older.

Yesterday
we took him to the vet,
said goodbye,
left him there.

He was so little.
The hole in my heart
is
so
big.

WEEK 6: ON THE GROUND

Take 5!

1. **Create a word cloud or Wordle of the poem text** and display the image before sharing the poem. (See the PFAMS blog for a ready-made word cloud version of the poem.) Then discuss the impact of the words in the shape of a poem versus as a Wordle.

2. **The two-stanza arrangement of this poem lends itself to reading aloud in two groups.** Invite two volunteers to choose a partner each and then have each pair read one stanza aloud. Encourage students to seek out an appropriate image on the web to display during their read-aloud. (You'll find one example at the website of the Australian [natural history] Museum at: australianmuseum.net.au.)

3. Sometimes poets weave facts into their poems. Guide students in noting what information we learn about bombardier beetles in this poem. Talk about how writers can share information in many formats, including poems or paragraphs. **Encourage students to seek out related nonfiction works or relevant websites** about this creature and talk about how writers use these two different formats to share information and communicate with an audience.

4. In this poem, **the poet uses the element of alliteration to repeat the same sound in the beginning of several words** for greater emphasis. Challenge students to locate examples of this (for example, the "b" sound in *bombardier beetle, big boiling blast*). Enterprising students may also notice the repeated presence of the "s" sound at the beginning and at the end of many words (*stink, expels; squirt, mace; predator's, face*).

5. Follow this poem about prey with a poem about a predator, **"The Shark" by X.J. Kennedy** (7th Grade, Week 7, page 117), or selections from Jane Yolen's photo-illustrated collection *Bug Off!: Creepy, Crawly Poems*.

Consider the Bombardier Beetle
by Jane Yolen

If grabbed by a frog
Or an ant or a toad
The bombardier beetle
Will almost explode.

The stink it expels
Like a squirt of bug mace
Is a big boiling blast
In the predator's face.

WEEK 7: IN THE WATER

Take 5!

1. The Loch Ness monster is the source of hundreds of years of speculation with little evidence or documentation. Still the legend persists, with several fuzzy images promoted as sightings of the creature. Find and **show one of those images before reading the poem and see if students guess the subject**, either before or after reading the poem. One source is Nessie.co.uk.

2. Since the location for this "monster" is a loch, or lake, in Scotland, see if anyone is brave enough to **try reading the poem with a Scottish accent**, just for fun—even just the opening and closing lines, which are the same line. Or collaborate with a speech or theater teacher (or local Scot) to provide a Scottish reading.

3. Research Loch Ness monster myths across the ages. **What similar stories have students heard about creatures in your area?**

4. **This is a "poem of address" or "apostrophe" poem in which the poet is speaking directly to the subject**. Poems of address can speak even to objects or animals as if they were human. Ask the students to find details from this poem that make it a poem of address, such as the salutation "Dear monster of Loch Ness" and the use of "you."

5. Revisit **"Locker Ness Monster" by Robyn Hood Black** (6th Grade, Week 2, page 31) to consider the pun Black employs ("Locker Ness" from "Loch Ness"). You might also share more poetry by Jack Prelutsky, such as selections from *Behold the Bold Umbrellaphant* or *The Swamps of Sleethe: Poems from Beyond the Solar System*.

DEAR MONSTER OF LOCH NESS
by Jack Prelutsky

Dear monster of Loch Ness,
You're not at your address,
We haven't seen you recently,
We miss you, more or less.
We wonder day and night
Why you are out of sight.
Dear monster, we sincerely hope
That everything's all right.

We like it when you're here,
And when you're not, we fear
That nothing will be fine until
You somehow reappear.
We openly confess
You're causing us distress.
For you we yearn, so please return,
Dear monster of Loch Ness.

WEEK 8: IN THE AIR

SIXTH GRADE

Take 5!

1. As a physical prop related to the poem, **place a "clean, clear" jar in front of you before reading this poem** aloud to heighten interest and make a concrete connection.

2. This "list" poem lends itself to incorporating six or more volunteers for the first six lines of the poem. **Invite six students to select their favorite line and to read it aloud,** alone or with a partner, while you read the final two lines aloud.

3. Here is an opportunity to **talk about simple science experiments or science fair projects** that students have tried in the past or might be interested in considering for the future. Look for nonfiction resource books by Vicki Cobb for examples.

4. The poet builds this "how to" poem line by line, revealing the subject of the poem at the end (lightning bug or firefly). **Guide the students in inferring what the poem is about based on each line of the poem,** beginning with the title. At what point are they certain about the poem's subject? Which details are most significant in drawing those conclusions?

5. Revisit **"Consider the Bombardier Beetle" by Jane Yolen** (6th Grade, Week 6, page 39) for another insect poem, or share selections from *Seeds, Bees, Butterflies and More!* by Carole Gerber.

Night Light
by Carole Gerber

A clean, clear jar.
A dark still night.
A time to wait.
A flash of light.
A quick, sure hand.
A gentle close.
A bug inside a jar
that glows.

WEEK 9: WEATHER

SIXTH GRADE

Take 5!

1. If a window is nearby, **take a few moments for some cloud watching** prior to reading this poem aloud. Or check out CloudAppreciationSociety.org for cloud images.

2. Share the poem aloud again and **invite students to join in on either line 12 or 13 (*I'll take a chance / and race the clouds*)**, lines that evoke the title of the poem, too.

3. **Survey students about their fitness preferences:** running, walking, hiking, martial arts, dance, soccer, yoga, and so on. Make a quick graph of the results.

4. Poets compare one thing to another using metaphors and similes to give us a fresh perspective on both things. **Lead the students in identifying the simile in this poem**: *Raindrops / wait with heavy breath, / like tense soldiers listening.* What two things are being compared to one another (raindrops, soldiers)?

5. For another poem about racing or chasing clouds, see **"Biking Along White Rim Road" by Irene Latham** (7th Grade, Week 3, page 109).

RACING THE CLOUDS
by Jacqueline Jules

The sky
is the color of a battleship.
Raindrops
wait with heavy breath,
like tense soldiers listening
for a general's barked command.
The battle
will begin tonight.
But now
the sidewalk summons,
and a warm breeze kisses my cheek.
I'll take a chance
and race the clouds.
Hear my heart pound
in rhythm with my feet.

WEEK 10: FOOD

SIXTH GRADE

Take 5!

1. Treat yourself to your favorite breakfast pastry! Set it out for view as a poetry prop before reading the poem. Then **read the poem aloud, savoring the food words, and take a bite of pastry** at the end.

2. Alert the students to all the food words in this poem (*pan dulce; Little Horns, Little Shells, Sandals, / Bowties, Braids, and Coco Cookies, / Little Corn, Little Pigs—; Cuernitos, Conchitas, Huaraches, Corbatas, / Trenzas, Cocadas, Elotitos, Cochinitos; Ojo de Buey, / the Eye of a Bull*). Display the words of the poem and **invite students to choose their favorite food word and chime in** when that word appears while you read the whole poem aloud again.

3. **Talk about other favorite pastries and baked goods** from all kinds of bakeries in your community.

4. Lead a discussion about the experience of reading or listening to this poem (when you read it aloud) in contrast with viewing a digital video adaptation of the poem. **Look for the "poem movie" featuring this poem** on the PFAMS blog (PFAMS.blogspot.com). Contrast what students "see" and "hear" when reading or listening to the poem to what they perceive when they watch the movie based on the poem.

5. Follow up with another poem celebrating food, **"Food Fest" by Heidi Bee Roemer** (8th Grade, Week 10, page 199), or contrast with **"The Café" by Guadalupe Garcia McCall** (8th Grade, Week 13, page 205). For cross-genre comparisons, share a selection from one of Gary Soto's short story collections such as *Facts of Life: Stories*.

NAMES
by Julie Larios

Saturday morning means I buy pan dulce
with Tio Chepe and my cousin Lucesita
whose name means "Little Light"—
that's what I call her, and she laughs
and pinches me and calls me "Peace"
because my name is Paz.

In the panaderia even the pastries
have names that mean other things:
Little Horns, Little Shells, Sandals,
Bowties, Braids, and Coco Cookies,
Little Corn, Little Pigs—
everything in Spanish sounds like a song:
Cuernitos, Conchitas, Huaraches, Corbatas,
Trenzas, Cocadas, Elotitos, Cochinitos.

Saturday mornings, Saturday mornings,
that's what I sing because I love pan dulce
and sometimes English can be a song, too.
*Tio Chepe, Tio Chepe, Uncle Joey, Uncle Joey,
buy me, please, an Ojo de Buey,
the Eye of a Bull on a Saturday morning!*

Tio Chepe picks out a bagful—
this one, that one, that one, this one,
while I sing, and Little Light flirts
with the boy behind the counter
whose name is Jesus.

WEEK 11: MORE FOOD

Take 5!

1. Set the stage for this unusual word puzzle poem by **writing a math formula on the board: x + y = z.** Then read the poem aloud very slowly with a long pause after each word in column 1.

2. First, students may want to talk about how the word in column 2 fits the prompt in column 1. Then **read the poem aloud again with you taking the lead in saying the words in column 1** and the students responding with the "answer," the newly coined word, in column 2.

3. **Brainstorm more examples of food-related "one-worders" in two columns** as Lewis demonstrates in his poem. You may want to start "backwards"—thinking of clever word puns and then deciding how to lead up to that answer with a descriptive phrase.

4. **Here the poet invites us to make inferences based on cue words, like solving a puzzle.** Lead students in discussing the problem-solving process. For example, "Macarooni" is based on the word "macaroon," a coconut cookie, plus the word "macaroni," a kind of pasta. Deconstruct each of the words in column 2 together with students.

5. For more one-worder fun, share **"One-Worders" by J. Patrick Lewis** (8th Grade, Week 26, page 231), or follow with "One-Worders" found in *If You Were a Chocolate Mustache,* also by J. Patrick Lewis.

FOOD ONE-WORDERS
by J. Patrick Lewis

Pasta-filled cookie → Macarooni
Green dog → Broccollie
Robin's snack → Earthwo—
Onion → Vegetaball
Look, a fly—no, it's . . . *Souperman!*

WEEK 12: HOUSE & HOME

SIXTH GRADE

Take 5!

1. Before sharing the poem aloud, **set an alarm clock or cell phone alarm** to launch the poem reading.

2. In a follow-up reading, form six groups of students and **challenge each group to research and find a short audio clip** for the sounds referenced in the poem (alarm clock, blow dryer, clothes dryer, toaster, tea kettle, microwave). Each group should take a different object/sound. (One source of sounds and sound effects is SoundCloud.com.) Then read the poem aloud again and invite each group to play its sound when it is mentioned in the poem. Make a podcast of the whole thing to save and play again later—perhaps on the school-wide morning announcements!

3. Invite students to share elements of their own morning routines. **What is the secret to getting ready fast?**

4. Sometimes poets use their imaginations to guess what it might be like if something that is not alive had a real personality—which is called **the element of personification.** Guide the students in determining which words or lines in this poem suggest that a house and the objects in the house are breathing beings (*My house wakes me up; my alarm clock starts dancing; the sounds of my house come alive; The blow dryer screams at the top of its lungs; My snooze alarm clock starts singing*).

5. Compare this poem with another descriptive poem about place: **"Her Room" by Laura Purdie Salas** (8th Grade, Week 12, page 203).

THE WAKING HOUSE
by Charles Ghigna

My house wakes me up every morning
Exactly at six forty-five—
That's when my alarm clock starts dancing
And the sounds of my house come alive.

The blow dryer screams at the top of its lungs,
The clothes dryer buzzer starts pinging.
I pull up the covers over my head.
My snooze alarm clock starts singing.

The toaster goes pop. When will it stop?
The tea kettle whistles away.
The microwave beep won't let me sleep,
I might as well join in the day.

WEEK 13: FAMILIES

SIXTH GRADE

Take 5!

1. Set the stage for sharing this poem by asking: Is poetry a piece of cake? A cake walk? Or the icing on the cake? Then read the poem aloud, **pausing briefly before each word or phrase in quotation marks.**

2. Sometimes poets use basic graphic elements and mechanical conventions like simple quotation marks to add interest to their poems. Guide students in discussing how quotation marks help show us how to read this poem. Then read the poem aloud together again, **inviting students to volunteer for the parts in quotation marks.**

3. For discussion: *What expressions or advice do your parents (or grandparents or others) offer?*

4. Sometimes poets use everyday or colloquial language in their poems for a particular effect. Work with students to **identify the poet's use of idioms**—an expression that is not meant to be taken literally, like "kicked the bucket." Examples in this poem include: *You'd better hold your tongue; You'd better watch your step; You're walking on thin ice; a loose cannon; play these games; worth a hill of beans.* Talk about both the literal and figurative meaning of each expression.

5. Connect this poem with another poem featuring an idiom, **"Another New Year" by Janet Wong** (7th Grade, Week 1, page 105).

THE POETRY FRIDAY ANTHOLOGY

MOM TALK
by Kristy Dempsey

Sometimes my mother calls me "smart."
I think she's telling lies.
She says, "You'd better hold your tongue,"
and when I do, she rolls her eyes.
"You better watch your step, my son.
You're walking on thin ice."
But when I look, the ground below
seems extra-firm and nice.
She calls me a "loose cannon,"
but I do not have a fuse.
She tells me not to "play these games,"
but it isn't win or lose.
I do not think my mother says
exactly what she means,
except when my "allowance won't be
worth a hill of beans!"

WEEK 14: COMMUNITY

Take 5!

1. Read this poem aloud using a quiet voice for the first four stanzas, but **read the final stanza louder and with confidence.**

2. **In a follow-up reading, focus on the second stanza** in particular, inviting students to choose one of the four lines to say while you read the whole poem aloud again.

3. **Survey students on sports they have experienced,** such as baseball, football, soccer, and basketball. Which of these sports do they think could be discussed in this particular poem?

4. Poets often use metaphors to compare one thing to another to give us a fresh perspective on both things. **Guide the students in identifying the metaphor in this poem**, with a focus on the second stanza, in particular. What two things are being compared to one another? (Being new = *an in-between place, / an invisible door / that turns outside to inside, / stranger to friend.*)

5. Revisit another sports-themed poem, **"Tryouts" by Jen Bryant** (6th Grade, Week 3, page 33), or follow with more poems about sports from *Good Sports: Rhymes about Running, Jumping, Throwing, and More* by Jack Prelutsky. For cross-genre comparisons, link this poem with any of Chris Crutcher's sports-themed short stories in *Athletic Shorts: Six Short Stories.*

First Practice
by Amy Ludwig VanDerwater

I'm new on this team
but I've been new before.

It's an in-between place,
an invisible door
that turns outside to inside,
stranger to friend.

It's the first day of practice.

I try to pretend
that my hands are not shaking.
I'm not scared at all.
I'll be tough on the field.
I'll go for the ball.

I'm new
but my teammates
are calling my name.
I've been new before.
I'm good at this game.

WEEK 15: STUFF WE LOVE

Take 5!

1. **Make a pile of crazy gifts from the little brother mentioned in the poem** (small stones, plastic magic rings, brussels sprouts, pennies, ladybugs, orange rinds, dandelions, ice cubes). Then read the poem aloud, picking up the objects (as many as you have) as each one is mentioned in the poem.

2. Read the poem aloud again, but this time **invite the students to choose one crazy gift line to read** while you read the rest of the poem out loud.

3. **Invite students to share funny stories about younger siblings.**

4. Point out that sometimes poets borrow the patterns from other things, like lists, for creating a new poem. **Work together to make a simple list of all the "gift" items mentioned in the poem.** Then contrast the simple list with the poet's arrangement and addition of words and phrases in the poem. Note that the poem has also used rhyme to unify the lines and stanzas.

5. Compare this with another poem in which the poet complains (lovingly) about a sibling: **"Dracula" by Carmen T. Bernier-Grand** (7th Grade, Week 17, page 137) or **"Movies of Us" by Michael J. Rosen** (8th Grade, Week 17, page 213).

GIVING
by Jane Yolen

I have a little brother
Who loves to give me things,
Like small stones from our driveway
And plastic magic rings.

He gives me all his brussels sprouts,
And pennies that he finds.
He loves to hand me ladybugs
And curling orange rinds.

He gives me dandelions,
And little cubes of ice.
And yesterday he brought from school
An itchy head of lice.

Oh, no,
Thanks, Bro.

WEEK 16: HOLIDAYS

Take 5!

1. Before reading this poem aloud, **show a menu from a Chinese or other Asian restaurant**.

2. **Invite three volunteers to research and find a short audio clip for the sounds referenced in the poem** (coins jingling, clock ticking, door bell ringing). One source of sounds and sound effects is SoundCloud.com. Then read the poem aloud again along with the sound effects as they are mentioned in the poem.

3. **Poll students on their favorite Thanksgiving foods or traditions.**

4. Sometimes poets use words that sound like sounds; this is called the element of *onomatopoeia*. **Challenge the students to identify the sound words in this poem** (*Jingle, jangle; tick tock; jingle, jangling; Ding dong*). Talk about what the sound words and sound effects add to the impact of the poem.

5. Follow this with another food-themed poem by **Janet Wong, "Community Service"** (8th Grade, Week 14, page 207), or compare this poem to "Albert J. Bell" in *A Suitcase of Seaweed*, also by Janet Wong.

WONG'S CAFÉ
by Janet Wong

My grandparents own a restaurant,
Wong's Café: Vermont and 8th.
Jingle, jangle—
do you hear the quarters in my apron pocket?
I take the orders and collect the tips.

Mr. Albert Bell (Mr. Beef Fried Rice)
and Mrs. Bell (his very pretty wife)
used to come here now and then.
But Al Bell's wife died a month ago.
And now he's here every single night.

Same time: *tick tock*, 6 o'clock on the dot.
Beef fried rice and a real good tip—
no *jingle, jangling*. Dollar bills, crisp dollar bills.

My grandmother (my PoPo) found out
that Al Bell was planning to stay at home
and eat a TV dinner, all by himself,
alone on Thanksgiving night.
She didn't want him home alone,
so she told him she'd never serve him again
if he didn't come and eat at our house.
Ding dong! There he is!

I open the door. He follows me.
And then I turn around and see
Al Bell's eyes pop out of his head
and he says he can't believe the *stuff* —
(stuff an all-American family would eat):
turkey and dressing, biscuits and yams,
cranberry sauce, pumpkin pie.

And just for him: a bowl of rice.

Week 17: Time Together

Take 5!

1. For a fun poetry prop, **place a fishing pole** by your desk or table before reading this poem **or find and display a photo of three generations** (if possible, a son, father, grandfather).

2. **Stage a "tableau," a frozen moment of the poem posed as a "scene,"** with student volunteers posing as described in the lines of the poem. Read the poem aloud, photograph and/or film the tableau, and post it with the poem.

3. For discussion: *How are we different from—and similar to—our parents?*

4. **Contrast the experience of reading or listening to this poem with viewing a digital movie version of the poem.** Look for the "poem movie" featuring this poem on the PFAMS blog (PFAMS.blogspot.com). What does each experience (reading, listening, viewing) offer that is unique?

5. Follow this with another fishing poem, **"Cod" by Holly Thompson** (8th Grade, Week 36, page 251), or selections from *Fishing with Dad: Lessons of Love and Lure from Father to Son* by Michael J. Rosen, or with the memoir poems of David L. Harrison in *Connecting Dots: Poems of My Journey*.

FISHING TRIP
by Charles Waters

8AM
Grandpa, Dad and I slump
in our aqua blue, flat-bottom skiff.
We've been here since sunrise
waiting to catch tonight's supper.
I wonder if I can finally earn my keep,
if I can live up to being
a third-generation fisherman.
I stare at myself in the water.
I feel a snap on the reel
and see my reflection turn into
a jigsaw puzzle blown to bits.
I spring into action, keeping tension
on the line while hauling in a halibut
spasming against the sun.
"Atta boy!" yells Grandpa.
Dad sports a grin so big
I notice that we smile alike.

WEEK 18: HUMAN BODY

SIXTH GRADE

Take 5!

1. If you're feeling brave, **show anatomy images—featuring the location of the appendix**—after reading this poem aloud.

2. Share the poem again, and this time **invite students to join in on the last line for emphasis** (*an appendectomy*).

3. Take a moment to **research a few facts about the appendix**, particularly the warning signs for appendicitis. One source is Medlineplus.gov.

4. Sometimes poets use their imaginations to guess what it might be like if something that is not alive had a real personality; this is called the element of personification. **Guide the students in determining which words or lines in this poem suggest an appendix is a breathing being** (*sly, lurks, sleeps, never works, lazy*, etc.).

5. Share another poem about body parts, **"Eviscerate" by Michael Salinger** (8th Grade, Week 33, page 245), or follow with more poems about the human body from *The Blood-Hungry Spleen and Other Poems About Our Parts* by Allan Wolf.

WEEK 18: HUMAN BODY

YOUR APPENDIX IS A MYSTERY
by **Allan Wolf**

Where large and small intestines meet
the sly appendix lurks.
It takes no part in anything.
It sleeps and never works.
It hangs about, this lazy worm,
no use to you or me.
The only thing that moves it is
an appendectomy!

Week 19: More Human Body

Take 5!

1. If possible, **get a Ping-Pong ball and draw an eye on it**—but don't let students see what you've done until after you've read the poem aloud and after they've guessed the answer to the riddle.

2. Do a bit of quick collaborative research on eyes, and **find and display an image of an eye while you read the poem aloud again.**

3. Sometimes poets weave facts into their poems. Guide students in noting what information we learn about the eye in this poem. Talk about how writers can share information in many formats, including poems or paragraphs. **Seek out related nonfiction works on this topic,** such as *Eyes and Ears* by Seymour Simon, and encourage students to consider how writers use these two formats to share information and communicate with an audience.

4. Point out that sometimes poets borrow the patterns from other things, like riddles, to create a new poem. **Guide students in identifying the clues that suggest the poem's subject** (*visible; small; size / of a Ping-Pong ball; clear salty liquid; washes; particle; folds of skin; shut*). Then read the poem again.

5. Connect this poem with **"Company" by Gail Carson Levine** (7th Grade, Week 22, page 147). Or for more riddles about science, see *Scien-Trickery: Riddles in Science* by J. Patrick Lewis.

A Light Reaction
by Carol-Ann Hoyte

Though my visible part
looks quite small,
I'm actually the size
of a Ping-Pong ball.
My clear salty liquid
washes away
particle strangers.
My folds of skin
automatically shut
to keep me from danger.

Answer: eye

Week 20: Art & Colors

Take 5!

1. Tape a sheet of paper to the board, or use a whiteboard, and **draw a picture** (a doodle or sketch suggested by the poem, such as weeds in a jar) while you read this poem aloud.

2. Read the poem aloud again, and **invite students to choose one thing to quick-sketch from this poem**. Create a quick collage of their sketches arranged around a copy of the poem to show the variety of possible poem interpretations.

3. **Talk with students about the artist mentioned in the poem, Vincent van Gogh**. Find and share an image of his famous *Sunflowers* painting or read selected facts from the nonfiction biography, *Vincent van Gogh: Portrait of an Artist* by Jan Greenberg and Sandra Jordan.

4. Poets compare one thing to another using similes to give us a fresh perspective on both things. **Lead the students in identifying the simile in this poem** (*like I was Vincent van Gogh / getting started on those sunflowers*). What two things are being compared to one another? Then read the poem aloud again.

5. Follow with another colorful art poem, **"Just Wanted to Tell You" by Patricia Hubbell** (7th Grade, Week 20, page 143), or share selections by Deborah Ruddell from *A Whiff of Pine, a Hint of Skunk: A Forest of Poems*.

WEEK 20: ART & COLORS

SIXTH GRADE ART CLASS
The First Day
by **Deborah Ruddell**

I was expecting to color rainbows
and sprinkle glitter on snowscenes
like we did back in fifth grade.
But I was in for a big surprise.

I found myself staring
at a bunch of weeds in a glass jar.
Learning the names of the weeds.
Studying their jagged leaves
and ragged petals.
Noticing their hairy stems.

Facing a sheet of yellowed paper
with a twig of charcoal in my hand.

My eyes open wide,
like I was Vincent van Gogh
getting started on those sunflowers.

WEEK 21: LOVE & FRIENDSHIP

Take 5!

1. Some students may not have been exposed to fairy tales in childhood. **Invite a student who is familiar with the Rapunzel fairy tale to summarize it** for the class before you read the poem aloud.

2. **Create an impromptu readers' theater performance of the poem.** Invite six volunteers to perform the poem, with all of them reading the opening and closing refrain in unison (the first three and last three lines of the poem). Then one at a time, each volunteer reads one two-line couplet of "advice" to Rapunzel. Be sure to read with plenty of attitude!

3. **Discuss with students other examples of fairy tale archetypes** (like Prince Charming) in modern times (an attractive guy). For example, are stepmothers today "wicked"? Are young men still selling everything for the possibility of magic beans, as in "Jack and the Beanstalk"? Consider characters from film and television adaptations of fairy tales as possible examples.

4. Sometimes poets include refrains of repeated text in their poems to give them a distinct structure. **Lead students in discussing the use of the refrain in this poem** (repeating the first three lines of the poem again at the end) to "bookend" the poem. Why might the poet have chosen this device for her opening and closing (to sound like a fairy tale, to reinforce her point about being cautious, etc.)?

5. Connect with **"The Boy" by Guadalupe Garcia McCall** (8th Grade, Week 22, page 223), or share poems from *Grumbles from the Forest* by Jane Yolen and Rebecca Kai Dotlich or *Mirror Mirror* by Marilyn Singer.

Advice to Rapunzel
by Eileen Spinelli

Rapunzel, Rapunzel, Rapunzel beware.
Be cautious and wise
when you let down your hair.
Who is this Prince Charming
who claims to be true?
Who claims to be caring for
nothing but you?
Be sure you're not blinded
by his gold and crown
before you go letting
your lovely hair down.
Is this prince a kind boy
who rides down the road?
Or is he a cad with
the heart of a toad?
Rapunzel, Rapunzel, Rapunzel beware.
Be cautious and wise
when you let down your hair.

WEEK 22: A KINDER PLACE

Take 5!

1. Before reading this poem (in a soft voice), **point out to students that many poems are funny, but some are serious**—like this one. Then read the poem in a quiet voice.

2. **Invite two volunteers to choose a partner each and then have each pair alternate reading** the four stanzas aloud with quiet voices.

3. For discussion: *How do you keep from saying (or texting) the wrong thing to a friend?*

4. Poets choose each word carefully as they craft their poems. **Lead the students in discussing the impact the words, line breaks, and even punctuation (and pauses) have on the meaning and tone of the poem.** How do you know this poem is sad? Then read the poem again.

5. Follow with another poem about lost friends, **"Season to Forgive" by Ken Slesarik** (7th Grade, Week 16, page 135), or share Langston Hughes's poem about losing a friend, "Poem" from *The Dream Keeper*.

LOST
by Kate Coombs

I lost a friend today.

I said some words
no one should say.

I watched her face change,
and then

I watched her walk
away.

WEEK 23: EXPLORING

Take 5!

1. After reading this poem aloud, **talk briefly about various modes of transportation** including ferries and camels—and the idea that a camel could serve as a "ferry" across the desert, much like a boat across a body of water.

2. **Invite students to research images or videos of dromedary camels and project those** while you read the poem aloud again. (One excellent source is the website Video.NationalGeographic.com.) Students can join in on the last two words of the poem (*but slow*) with exaggerated slowness.

3. Sometimes poets weave facts into their poems. **Guide students in noting what information we learn about dromedary camels in this poem.** Talk about how writers can share information in many formats, including poems or paragraphs. Contrast with the informational book, *My Librarian Is a Camel: How Books Are Brought to Children Around the World* by Margriet Ruurs.

4. Poets often use sensory language to create imagery. **Talk with students about how active verbs and descriptive adjectives are used** in this poem to paint a picture in your mind (*skims, sea of sand, step by step, lush oasis, fierce wind roaring, camels snoring*, etc.). After this discussion, share the whole poem aloud again.

5. Compare this safe (but slow) mode of transportation to an unsafe (but lucky) driving experience with the poem **"Black Ice" by Joseph Bruchac** (7th Grade, Week 34, page 171), or read another poem on transportation by Juanita Havill, "Wheel of Progress" (*The Poetry Friday Anthology K-5 Edition*; 5th Grade, Week 24).

Dromedary Ferry
by Juanita Havill

The dromedary ferry
skims across the sea of sand,
the surest way to travel
in an empty desert land.

Step by step through changing dunes,
each patient dromedary paces.
Mystery of navigation
leading to a lush oasis.

Sleep in tents beneath the stars
protected from the fierce wind roaring.
When at last the wind dies down,
listen to the camels snoring.

The dromedary ferry
is the only way to go
across the shifting desert sands.
It's safe and secure—but slow.

Note: Sand is not water and a camel caravan is not exactly a ferry boat, and yet camels transport people and goods across the desert.

WEEK 24: SCIENCE & TECHNOLOGY

SIXTH GRADE

Take 5!

1. **As a simple poetry prop, place your cell phone quietly down** in front of the students as you read the poem aloud slowly.

2. Work with students to **create a quick graphic "novel" rendering of the poem** with five panels, one for each line of the poem (e.g., one quick cartoon sketch and speech bubble for *I sent you a text*, one for *and when you sent me one back*, etc.). Then read the poem aloud again, displaying the poem alongside the graphic "novel" version.

3. For discussion: *Which is worse, waiting for a text message that may never come or sending an inappropriate text message?*

4. Poets choose and arrange each word carefully as they craft their poems. Guide the students in discussing the impact of the words, line breaks, and punctuation, or lack of it, on the poem. Contrast this with a **look at the poem as if it were written as continuous prose** (*I sent you a text and when you sent me one back the teacher caught us now you're not speaking to me my phone is silent*). Although those 118 characters might fit into a Tweet, Kulp has created a poignant poem by her structural choices.

5. Revisit **"Lost" by Kate Coombs** (6th Grade, Week 22, page 71), another poem about tension in friendship, or select excerpts from one of Lauren Myracle's epistolary novels featuring texting and instant messaging, such as *ttyl*.

THE POETRY FRIDAY ANTHOLOGY

WEEK 24: SCIENCE & TECHNOLOGY

SIXTH GRADE

SILENCE
by **Linda Kulp**

I sent you a text
and when you sent me one back
the teacher caught us—
now you're not speaking to me
my phone is silent

WEEK 25: SONG & DANCE

Take 5!

1. In this poem about preparing for a performance, the narrator is struggling with a costume and props. So, to add some humor to your reading, **create a simple costume out of whatever you have available** and pantomime the actions described in the poem as you read it aloud.

2. Read the poem aloud again and **invite two student volunteers to shine flashlights or other lights on you when you get to the final line** (*lights shine on me*). Pause beforehand for greater emphasis. (Keep a flashlight handy for next week's poem.)

3. **Invite students to share their experiences with live theater,** either as performers or as audience members.

4. Poets give their poems shape and structure in many ways. **Talk with students about how the short lines and line breaks give this very vertical poem a distinctive rhythm.** Note that the poet has also set the last line apart for greater emphasis. Consider the poet's use of rhyme, too, including end rhyme (*pin/chin; prop/flop; legs/eggs; wings/rings; pee/me*) and "slant" or "almost" rhyme (*lines/fine*).

5. For another poem about performance jitters, see **"I Had a Nightmare" by April Halprin Wayland** (8th Grade, Week 19, page 217).

OPENING NIGHT
by **Renée M. LaTulippe**

Costume broke,
can't find a pin.
My makeup's running
down my chin.
Who took my wig?
Is that my prop?
(You think we'll be
a giant flop?)
Butterflies
and noodle legs.
Terrified
of hurtled eggs.
What if I
forget my lines?
(Stop it now!
You're fine, you're FINE!)
Waiting (QUIET!)
in the wings.
Five deep breaths.
Warning bell rings.
Curtain rises.
(Gotta pee!)
I step on stage—

lights shine on me.

WEEK 26: NONSENSE

SIXTH GRADE

Take 5!

1. **Create or show a shadow** with a flashlight, if needed, as you read the poem aloud.

2. Stage a "tableau"—a frozen moment of the poem posed as a "scene"—to accompany another reading of this poem. **Ask for two student volunteers, one posing as the narrator as described in the poem and one posing as the shadow** while you read the poem aloud again.

3. For discussion: *What might be your own shadow's favorite food?*

4. **Sometimes poets use exaggeration to add impact to their poems. This use of figurative language is called hyperbole.** Discuss this element with students and identify its use in this poem (the characterization of the shadow eating and "hogging" food, the shadow quickly "gaining" eight pounds while the narrator loses eight pounds, and the narrator disappearing, etc.). Why did the poet use hyperbole in this way in this poem? Then read the poem aloud again.

5. For another fun poem about eating, see **"What I Want to Be" by Mary Quattlebaum** (7th Grade, Week 10, page 123).

WEEK 26: NONSENSE

MERE SHADOW
by Robert Weinstock

My shadow secretly grew tired
Of eating shadow food,
And now it's hogging all of *my*
Food too . . . this isn't good.

Since Saturday it's gained eight pounds,
While I weigh eight pounds less.
I'm starting to hallucinate
From hunger, I confess.

At this rate I am worried I
Will slowly disappear.
Mere months from now you'll simply see
My shadow sitting here.

WEEK 27: WORLD OF WORDS

Take 5!

1. After sharing the poem aloud, talk about the unusual title, "Ack!"—an exclamation. **Make a quick list of familiar exclamations** (Oh! Aha!, etc.) and talk about appropriate vs. inappropriate exclamations (in different social contexts).

2. Share the poem out loud again, but **invite two or three students to join in on the last line for greater emphasis** (*too bad the moment's passed*).

3. **Look for advice columns in newspapers and magazines** or online. What do they recommend when it comes to saying the right thing at the right time?

4. **Guide students in analyzing how the poet creates humor in this poem**, beginning with the unusual title, the bragging over-statements, and the surprising contradiction in the final line. Consider how each of the poem's lines and stanzas contribute to the development of the poem's humor. Then read the poem aloud again.

5. Follow with another poem about dealing with conflict, **"The Fear Factor" by Sara Holbrook** (7th Grade, Week 33, page 169).

Ack!
by Cynthia Cotten

I always know just what to say.
The perfect words are there—
words that render others speechless,
uttered with such flair.

My comments are insightful,
my wit is unsurpassed.
Oh, yes, I know just what to say—
too bad the moment's passed.

WEEK 28: BOOKS

SIXTH GRADE

Take 5!

1. While you read this poem aloud, hold up a thesaurus. After sharing the poem, **give a quick lesson on how to use a thesaurus** or Thesaurus.com.

2. **Invite two volunteers to participate in a follow-up read-aloud that highlights the multiple synonyms** in many of the lines. You read the first part of each line (*I sound like a lizard*) while the first volunteer reads the second part of each line (*a dino*) and the second volunteer reads the third or final part of each line (*or fossil*). Note that only a few lines do not offer multiple synonyms, such as lines 3, 12, 14, 15, and 16.

3. **Challenge students to think of not one, but two synonyms** for each of the words on the weekly list of spelling or vocabulary words, or use National Spelling Bee words (found at SpellingBee.com).

4. Sometimes poets use their imaginations to guess what it might be like if something that is not alive had a real personality; this is called personification. **Guide the students in determining which words or lines in this "mask" poem suggest a thesaurus is a breathing being** (use of first person "I," and the concluding lines: *for I am The Saurus, Synonymous Rex, / King Onomasticon! Extinct? No way!*)

5. Follow up with a poem about spelling, **"Breaking the Spell" by Debbie Levy** (7th Grade, Week 27, page 157), or selections from *Well Defined: Vocabulary in Rhyme* by Michael Salinger.

MEET THE SAURUS
by Heidi Mordhorst

I sound like a lizard, a dino or fossil;
Instead I'm a reference, a volume, a book.
If you need some help or require assistance,
check in for a peek, a perusal or look.

I'm small, undersized, miniscule or compact
but I'm powerful, potent, I'm mighty or strong.
Please trust in, rely on, depend on, believe me—
I won't misinform or mislead, steer you wrong.

When you need to state or express or convey
a specific idea or notion or thought,
I can offer, propose, recommend or suggest
the word or expression that hits the right spot.

See me for that nuance, that hint or that shade
of meaning that captures what you want to say,
for I am The Saurus, Synonymous Rex,
King Onomasticon! Extinct? No way!

WEEK 29: POETRY POEMS

Take 5!

1. Before reading this poem aloud, **display a "newspaper blackout" poem**—a newspaper article or page with all the words blacked out EXCEPT the words that make up the "found" poem. These kinds of "found" poems are available in *Newspaper Blackout* by Austin Kleon and at his website, AustinKleon.com.

2. For a follow-up reading, **invite three volunteers to join you.** (They can each choose a partner if needed for extra confidence.) You read the first couplet and the final four couplets. Volunteer 1 reads the second couplet, Volunteer 2 reads the third couplet, and Volunteer 3 reads the fourth and fifth couplets.

3. **Collaborate with students to make a quick "found" poem out of a handful of the words in THIS poem.** Start with the same first line (*I'm sure there's a found poem somewhere here*) and then build a poem together by selecting words, phrases, or lines from the rest of the poem.

4. Poets enjoy experimenting with writing poetry in different forms and formats. One modern approach that is gaining momentum is the "found" poem. **A found poem is built upon the words from another source**, usually text from a non-poetic source like a newspaper article. Guide the students in talking about the several found poems Wayland mentions in her poem, as well as the process of creating such found poetry *from words that have trampolined / off an Internet ad or a magazine.*

5. For an example of a "found" poem, see **"Her Room" by Laura Purdie Salas** (8th Grade, Week 12, page 203). For more about found poems, see Georgia Heard's anthology *The Arrow Finds Its Mark*. For a different approach, contrast this poem about a figurative forest with poems about a literal forest from *Forest Has a Song* by Amy Ludwig VanDerwater.

IN THE WORD WOODS
by April Halprin Wayland

I'm sure there's a found poem somewhere here.
There usually is this time of year.

Didn't a red-haired boy lose words
that were found last May by a flightless bird?

And then that search and rescue hound
dug up sixteen poems he'd found.

Listen for falling bulletin boards,
and scowling poem-poaching hordes

who stomp all over this hallowed ground
until the hidden poems are found.

I'll bring a flashlight, you bring a rake
we'll get down on our knees and make

a poem from words that have trampolined
off an Internet ad or a magazine

into the woods some starry night
waiting for searching kids who might

find a poem if they're brave and follow
the hoot of an owl to the end of the hollow.

Week 30: Rhyme, Repetition, & Rhythm

Sixth Grade

Take 5!

1. While you read this poem aloud, **hold up a mug or cup of hot coffee, tea, or water.**

2. **Invite four volunteers to join you in reading the poem aloud again.** Each volunteer takes one of the four lines beginning with "hot" (*Hot air; hot rocks; hot water; hot words*).

3. Sometimes poets weave facts into their poems. **Guide students in noting what information we learn about convection in this poem.** Do a bit of quick collaborative research on the properties of convection.

4. **Lead students in considering the craft and structure of this poem**: how the words are arranged on the page, the length of each line, and where the poet has chosen to put the line breaks. What effect does this have on reading the poem? Then read the poem aloud again.

5. Revisit **"Ack!" by Cynthia Cotten** (6th Grade, Week 27, page 81) about saying the right words, or follow with selections from *This Is Just to Say: Poems of Apology and Forgiveness,* also by Joyce Sidman.

Convection
by **Joyce Sidman**

Hot air
    (on sun-baked hills),
hot rocks
    (from molten depths),
hot water
    (in a stove-top pot),
hot words
    (between friends),
all
rise,
erupt,
cool:

the convection rule.

WEEK 31: DIFFERENT FORMS

Take 5!

1. **Use the American Sign Language (ASL) alphabet to make the first letter of each line** as you read the poem aloud. One source is American Sign Language University at Lifeprint.com.

2. **Invite students to join in on using American Sign Language** to make the alphabet letters for each initial letter in each line of the poem while you read the poem aloud again.

3. **Poll students about their favorite after-school sports and graph the results.**

4. Sometimes poets use each of the letters of a key word to begin the lines of the poem; this is called acrostic poetry. **Highlight the first word of each line** in this poem, verbally and/or with ASL, to show how the letters of two words (*HOOPSTER HOPES*) were used, and talk about how those words echo the theme of the poem. Then read the poem aloud again.

5. Compare the acrostic form in this poem with **Avis Harley's** invented "intravista" form used in **"The Run"** (8th Grade, Week 3, page 185), or follow with more acrostic poems by Avis Harley in *African Acrostics: A Word in Edgeways*.

WEEK 31: DIFFERENT FORMS

FUTURE HOOPSTERS
by **Avis Harley**

Hour after hour
Out in the park
Or in the back lane
Playing 'til dark,
Shooting
The ball for that net reward—
Echoes of
Rebounds sound off the board!

Honing
Our skills,
Perfecting the aim—
Embracing the dream that
Shines through the game.

WEEK 32: METAPHOR & SIMILE

SIXTH GRADE

Take 5!

1. Read this poem aloud slowly, beginning with the title (which is part of the poem), and with dramatic pauses before each stanza. **Present it in a straight-forward, neutral tone of voice.**

2. **Then invite two volunteers to read the poem again.** (They can each choose a partner if needed for extra confidence.) Challenge one student or pair to read it in a very serious, quiet voice and the other student or pair to read it in an exaggerated, humorous tone of voice.

3. For discussion: *When is it brave to rock the boat and when is it unwise?*

4. Here **the poet invites us to make our own inferences** about what she (the poet) might be referring to—a broken friendship, an irritating moment, an angry fight, and so on. The meaning depends on understanding the phrase "Don't rock the boat." Discuss how this idiom is employed in parts (the title "That Boat" and the phrase *not / to rock*) and what it might mean in this context. Challenge students to support their opinions with specific words from the poem.

5. Contrast this figurative boat with a literal boat by revisiting **"Fishing Trip" by Charles Waters** (6th Grade, Week 17, page 61), or follow with another poem by **George Ella Lyon, "Saved by the Book"** (7th Grade, Week 29, page 161).

WEEK 32: METAPHOR & SIMILE

SIXTH GRADE

THAT BOAT
by **George Ella Lyon**

you
told me
not
to rock

sank

a long
time
ago.

WEEK 33: PERSONIFICATION

SIXTH GRADE

Take 5!

1. Hold up a pen while reading this poem aloud. If possible, **do a bit of scribbling on paper while reading** the poem and then end by putting the cap on the pen.

2. Invite two students to choose a partner and plan their reading of the two stanzas—**one stanza for each pair of volunteers**. Make a podcast of their reading.

3. For discussion: *What complaints might a computer keyboard, cell phone, or e-tablet have?*

4. Sometimes poets use their imaginations to guess what it might be like if something that is not alive had a real personality; this is called the element of personification. **Guide the students in determining how the poet suggests a pen is a breathing being** (use of "my" and "me," *pen that speaks*, etc.).

5. Compare the tattoos in this poem with the tattoos in **"Body Art" by Marilyn Singer** (8th Grade, Week 35, page 249), or read more poems by Nikki Grimes in *Planet Middle School*. For aspiring writers, suggest Ralph Fletcher's book, *A Writing Kind of Day*, full of poems and tips about creating poetry.

PEN
by Nikki Grimes

*Noisy people
leave their inky tattoos
on my white page
or squeeze their way
between the lines
of my yellow pad.
They tell me
who they are
what they think
what river of words
they want to ride.*

Have you ever tried
to put the cap
back on a pen
that speaks?
When I try
these stubborn voices
squeak.

WEEK 34: ON THE MOVE

SIXTH GRADE

Take 5!

1. Before reading this poem aloud, **show images of local historic markers and city signs** and ask students to guess what this poem might be about. (For example, Google "historic markers" for your town.)

2. **Alert the students to the place names in this poem** (*Solid Rock Church of Kerrville, Solid Rock, Comfort*) along with the final word of the poem (*slow*) and invite volunteers to chime in on those words only for greater emphasis.

3. **Encourage students to share sightings of other odd or funny signs or markers.**

4. **Collaborate with students to use Glogster.com to create a quick glog**, a digital interactive poster that pulls together images related to key words from the poem in a new, visual representation of the poem's theme. Talk with students about how the poet uses dramatic irony to make a point (Solid Rock has moved; Comfort isn't comforting, and so on). Then read the poem aloud again.

5, Read another **Naomi Shihab Nye** poem that employs irony, **"Editorial Suggestions"** (8th Grade, Week 27, page 233), and see more poems about Texas in *Is This Forever, or What?: Poems and Paintings from Texas*, edited by Naomi Shihab Nye.

THE POETRY FRIDAY ANTHOLOGY

TEXAS, OUT DRIVING
by Naomi Shihab Nye

The Solid Rock Church of Kerrville
has moved to another location.
It says so on the sign under
the name—Solid Rock.

Also the entire town of Comfort
appears to be for sale.
This does not feel comforting at all.

How many times we drove these curves,
pale fence posts, bent cedars . . .
but nothing needs us here.
Nothing we said, thought, forgot,
took root in the ditch around the bend.
I always want to stop at historic markers,
see what happened long before, but
the pull of motion keeps a car going,
passing by till next time,
which soon won't come,
even when everything we know
says *slow*.

Week 35: Summer Vacation

Take 5!

1. To set the stage for reading this poem aloud, **display group photos of extended families.** If you don't have any handy and want to share some hilarious examples, try AwkwardFamilyPhotos.com.

2. The arrangement of lines in this poem lends itself to a "call and response" read-aloud. **Break the students into two groups**—one will read the first line in the couplet stanza, and the other will read the second line of the couplet stanza. Then switch groups and read the poem aloud again.

3. **Invite students to share some of their favorite summer activities or plans.**

4. Talk with students about each stanza in this poem and how **the poet uses two-line stanzas (couplets) while maintaining the rhyme scheme across two couplets** (or four lines). Lead students in identifying each pair of rhyming words (*eggs/legs; dawn/lawn; free/me*).

5. Revisit another poem about cousins, **"Names" by Julie Larios** (6th Grade, Week 10, page 47), or go even further and share the opening pages of Virginia Hamilton's popular novel, *Cousins*.

COUSINS
by Charles Waters

Making breakfast—
Scrambled eggs,

Mosquito bites
On our legs,

Gazing at stars
Until dawn,

Playing soccer
On our lawn:

Every summer
We are free

To rule the world—
You and me.

WEEK 36: LOOKING FORWARD

Take 5!

1. **Create a simple poem prop similar to a highway sign featuring the word "Somewhere"** as if it were a town or city. Read the poem aloud and display the "Somewhere" sign during the reading.

2. For a choral reading, **coach the students to read only the first line of each of the first three stanzas** (*I know I'm going somewhere; I'm leaving soon for somewhere; I'm sure I'm going somewhere*) while you read the rest of the poem aloud.

3. Working together, **make a list of "somewhere" places that students would like to visit.**

4. Repetition is a key ingredient in creating many poems. **Sometimes a poet uses repetition not just to enhance the sound of the poem, but for meaning and emphasis.** Lead the students in discussing how the poet repeats both the use of the word "somewhere" and a similar kind of opening line for the first three stanzas (*I know I'm going somewhere; I'm leaving soon for somewhere; I'm sure I'm going somewhere*). Then read the poem aloud together again.

5. For another poem about exploring unknown territory, revisit **"In the Word Woods" by April Halprin Wayland** (6th Grade, Week 29, page 85), or share end-of-the-year poems from *Countdown to Summer* by J. Patrick Lewis. Collaborate with students to create a fun summer reading list, and be sure to include fiction, nonfiction and, of course, poetry!

I Know I'm Going Somewhere
by Ted Scheu

I know I'm going somewhere,
and I can hardly wait.
Somewhere's not the sort of place
where someone should be late.

I'm leaving soon for somewhere.
I'll ride my bike, I guess.
It all depends where somewhere is—
if it is far, or less.

I'm sure I'm going somewhere.
I'm finally on my way.
I hope I find that it's the kind
of place I'd like to stay.

I wish I had directions
to show me how to go.
If you've been somewhere recently
please call and let me know.

Why, we could go together there,
around each bump and bend.
Somewhere seems much closer
when you go there with a friend.

*"Poetry is most poetry when it **makes noise**."*

❧ Donald Hall ☙

Poems for Seventh Grade

POETRY TEKS FOR SEVENTH GRADE
(110.19. (b) (4); (8); (15 B i, ii, iii))

In **grade seven,** we focus on helping students understand:

- the structure and elements of poetry
- making inferences and drawing conclusions about poems
- supporting opinions with evidence from the poem
- how figurative language (such as personification, idioms, and hyperbole) contributes to meaning
- how a poet uses sensory language to create imagery
- determining the figurative meaning of phrases
- how the poet uses language to suggest mood
- the importance of graphic elements (e.g., capital letters, line length, word position) on the meaning of a poem
- how poets use rhyme scheme and meter in distinctive ways

SEVENTH GRADE

week 1	School	Another New Year *by Janet Wong*
week 2	More School	What She Asked *by Virginia Euwer Wolff*
week 3	Fun & Games	Biking Along White Rim Road *by Irene Latham*
week 4	Pets	Goldfish *by Joan Bransfield Graham*
week 5	More Pets	Monday's Cat *by Michael J. Rosen*
week 6	On the Ground	Feather *by Marilyn Singer*
week 7	In the Water	The Shark *by X.J. Kennedy*
week 8	In the Air	Spiral Glide *by Mary Lee Hahn*
week 9	Weather	After the Blizzard, Outside My Window *by Lesléa Newman*
week 10	Food	What I Want to Be *by Mary Quattlebaum*
week 11	More Food	Saying No *by Amy Ludwig VanDerwater*
week 12	House & Home	Fixer-Upper *by Terry Webb Harshman*
week 13	Families	Grandma's House *by Kate Coombs*
week 14	Community	Sitting for Trishie Devlin *by Sonya Sones*
week 15	Stuff We Love	These Hands *by Renée M. LaTulippe*
week 16	Holidays	Season to Forgive *by Ken Slesarik*
week 17	Time Together	Dracula *by Carmen T. Bernier-Grand*
week 18	Human Body	How Tall Is the Boy? *by Joy Acey*
week 19	More Human Body	Who Am I? *by Margarita Engle*
week 20	Art & Colors	Just Wanted to Tell You *by Patricia Hubbell*
week 21	Love & Friendship	Look My Way *by Robyn Hood Black*
week 22	A Kinder Place	Company *by Gail Carson Levine*
week 23	Exploring	The World According to Climbers *by Irene Latham*
week 24	Science & Tech	Gear *by Michael Salinger*
week 25	Song & Dance	The Deaf Boy *by Marilyn Nelson*
week 26	Nonsense	In the Bog *by Calef Brown*
week 27	World of Words	Breaking the Spell *by Debbie Levy*
week 28	Books	Wilbur Asks Charlotte Ten Questions *by Jane Yolen*
week 29	Poetry Poems	Saved by the Book *by George Ella Lyon*
week 30	RR&R	Fourths of Me *by Betsy Franco*
week 31	Different Forms	Mangoes *by Lesléa Newman*
week 32	Metaphor & Simile	Ars Poetica *by Georgia Heard*
week 33	Personification	The Fear Factor *by Sara Holbrook*
week 34	On the Move	Black Ice *by Joseph Bruchac*
week 35	Summer Vacation	Bilingual *by Margarita Engle*
week 36	Looking Forward	World Cup *by Jen Bryant*

WEEK 1: SCHOOL

Take 5!

1. Before presenting this back-to-school poem, **display one or two contrasting school photos of yourself from the past** (e.g., in school groups or teams or in after-school activities), if you have them. Or look for vintage photos of students from years gone by on Shorpy.com.

2. **Collaborate with students to use Glogster.com to create a quick glog**, a digital interactive poster that pulls together images (short haircut, the color red, guitars and bands, cross-country runner, brass ring) and key words (new, join, grab the brass ring) from the poem in a new, visual representation of the poem's theme (new starts, trying new things).

3. **Brainstorm a list of in-school and after-school activities** that are offered on your campus for students to consider.

4. Poets arrange their words and lines in a variety of ways to give a poem a certain rhythm and to add to its meaning. Here, **the poet uses a series of two-line couplets for each stanza and mixes rhymed and unrhymed lines.** Guide students in identifying the end rhymes (*thing/ring*), "slant" or "almost" rhymes (*start/short; today/train*), and unrhymed couplets (ending with *red/everyone; guitar/band*) and talk about how they make the poem sound. Then read the poem aloud again.

5. Follow up with another optimistic poem about a new start: **"First Practice" by Amy Ludwig VanDerwater** (6th Grade, Week 14, page 55).

ANOTHER NEW YEAR
by Janet Wong

Another new year:
another new start.

I'm thinking I should
cut my hair short.

And try wearing red.
Bright loud red

and not blend in
with everyone.

For fun I could learn
to play the guitar.

(Pull friends into
a small garage band?)

Our cross-country team
is meeting today.

I guess I could join.
I'd need to train.

I'll run every night till
I can't see a thing.

This is the year
I grab the brass ring.

WEEK 2: MORE SCHOOL

SEVENTH GRADE

Take 5!

1. Before reading this poem aloud, **fold a paper airplane as your poetry prop**. Then read the poem aloud and let your airplane fly.

2. **Share the poem aloud again, and this time invite one student volunteer to read the lines in quotation marks** spoken by the teacher in the poem *("Who in this whole room / can fly a paper airplane the highest?")*. Invite the rest of the students to chime in on the final line (*And every one of us did*) while you read the rest of the poem as narrator.

3. Students will almost certainly want to **fold and fly a paper airplane after reading this poem. Graph the results of whose airplane flies where** and then post the planes alongside a copy of the poem. For help, look for Seymour Simon's classic how-to book, *The Paper Airplane Book,* or *The World Record Paper Airplane Book* by Ken Blackburn and Jeff Lammers.

4. Sometimes poets use their imaginations to guess what it might be like if something that is not alive had a real personality; this is called the element of personification. **Guide the students in determining which words or lines in this poem personify inanimate objects as living, breathing beings** (*stubborn pens; misbehaving software staring back; The wall told us; sullen, pocked ceiling squares*). What does this element add to the tone of the poem? (Answers include heightening the sense that "*every big and every little thing / was wrong,*" even things without feelings.)

5. Share another poem about a stubborn pen, **"Pen" by Nikki Grimes** (6th Grade, Week 33, page 93), or selections from Virginia Euwer Wolff's *Make Lemonade*.

What She Asked
by Virginia Euwer Wolff

Remember that classroom afternoon,
every big and little thing
was wrong: Sleet outside, radiator clank within,
broken chalk, stubborn pens,
misbehaving software staring back.
The wall told us in its blunt rasp
about another bus delay.
Minds lolling, girls moody, guys grouchy,
we'd have tried on dour if we'd ever heard of it.
Even the boy who was memorizing pi
had dimmed his lights.
Marooned on the crust of that mopey day
our teacher looked around at all 38 of us
and up at the sullen, pocked ceiling squares
and wondered softly,
"Who in this whole room
can fly a paper airplane the highest?"
And every one of us did.

WEEK 3: FUN & GAMES

SEVENTH GRADE

Take 5!

1. **Display a cloud image (as big as you can make it) as a backdrop for reading this poem aloud.** (Check out CloudAppreciationSociety.org for cloud images.)

2. **The arrangement of lines in this poem lends itself to a "call and response" read aloud of the poem.** Break the students into two groups—one will read the first line in the couplet stanza, and the other will read the second line of the couplet stanza, with everyone reading the final line. Then switch groups and read it aloud again.

3. **Invite students to share their experiences with bicycling:** non-riders, occasional riders, experienced cyclists, competitive cyclists, and so on.

4. Poets give their poems shape and structure in many ways. **Talk with students about how the short lines and line breaks give this very vertical poem a distinctive rhythm.** Consider the poet's use of rhyme, too, including end rhyme (*jump/bump; jolt/bolt; loop/swoop; pace/race*), internal rhyme (*pace/race/chase*), and slant rhyme (*spin/descend/islands; parched/arches*).

5. Follow with another poem about a day of biking, **"A Perfect Day" by Julie Larios** (8th Grade, Week 20, page 219). For a cross-genre connection, watch a clip of a TED talk featuring professor Shimon Shocken sharing his experiences leading bike rides with juvenile inmates in Israel. Here's the link: Ted.com/talks/shimon_schocken_s_rides_of_hope.html.

BIKING ALONG WHITE RIM ROAD
by **Irene Latham**

We jump
        jolt

as wheels bump
        bolt.

We spin
        descend

across mesa-topped
        islands.

We loop
        swoop,

fly past parched
        arches.

We keep pace,
        race

chase schooling clouds.

WEEK 4: PETS

Take 5!

1. Before reading this poem, **find an image of a nasturtium (flower) and display it while sharing the poem aloud**. One source is the famed Burpee seed catalog online at Burpee.com.

2. Next, **collaborate with students to find a quick image of a goldfish that parallels your picture of the nasturtium**. Project both images as you read the poem aloud again, pausing briefly before the last three lines. Display a copy of the poem along with both images in a mini-collage.

3. **Open the floor to students who might want to share childhood memories** of pet funerals or a pet's death.

4. Here the poet invites us to make our own inferences about what she (the poet) might be referring to—the death of the goldfish, its decomposition in the earth, and the blossoming of a flower of a similar color to the goldfish. **Challenge students to identify which words or lines in the poem are most essential for understanding these elements.**

5. Read another poem about the loss of a pet, **"He Was So Little" by David L. Harrison** (6th Grade, Week 5, page 37).

Goldfish
by **Joan Bransfield Graham**

We found
you
floating
on your side—
iridescent
scales—
your fins
now still.
We buried you
in the flower
bed so
next year
you will
return,
you'll become...
orange
poppy,
nasturtium.

WEEK 5: MORE PETS

Take 5!

1. Read this poem aloud with particular emphasis on the days of the week. Afterward, **alert students to the fact that this poem is based on a very old rhyme called "Monday's Child,"** considered a tool for helping children learn the days of the week as well as predicting their dispositions based on the day of the week on which they were born. Look up a version of this original rhyme, if time allows.

2. **Work with students to create a quick graphic "novel" rendering of the poem with seven panels**, one for each day of the week mentioned in the poem (e.g., one quick cartoon sketch and speech bubble for "Monday's cat," one for "Tuesday's cat," and so on). Then read the poem aloud again, displaying the poem alongside the graphic "novel" version.

3. **Poll students on what days of the week they were born and quickly graph the results.**

4. Point out that **sometimes poets borrow patterns from other forms of writing to create a parody or humorous variation** of a previous work. Here, the poet has borrowed from an old nursery rhyme, "Monday's Child." Guide students in identifying the parallels between the two (using days of the week and personal attributes) and how the poet has captured the personalities of cats using that framework. Encourage students to pinpoint key words and phrases from the poem to support their observations.

5. Follow this poem based on a nursery rhyme with another poem based on a fairy tale, **"Advice to Rapunzel" by Eileen Spinelli** (6th Grade, Week 21, page 69), or by reading selections from *A Curious Collection of Cats* by Betsy Franco. For an additional connection, share "Black Cat" and other superstition poems from *Knock on Wood: Poems about Superstitions* by Janet Wong.

MONDAY'S CAT
by Michael J. Rosen

Monday's cat is full of mole.
Tuesday's cat has halved a vole.
Wednesday's cat has chipmunk breath,
Thursday's cat is mouse's death.
Friday's cat is munching warbler.
Saturday's cat ate something horribler.
But the cat who is born on Sunday's lap
is plump and happy and prone to nap.

Week 6: On the Ground

Take 5!

1. If possible, **bring a feather as a poetry prop to add a concrete connection to the poem**, or simply create a feather prop out of cut paper, fringed like a feather. Read the poem aloud and then display a copy of the poem along with the feather.

2. **For a follow-up reading, invite two volunteers to join you.** (They can each choose a partner if needed for extra confidence.) One volunteer or pair reads the first line (*A hawk flies by*), a second volunteer or pair reads the first phrase in the second line (*A feather lands*), and you read the rest of the poem aloud.

3. For discussion: *What would the grass tell the feather?*

4. Poets choose and arrange each word carefully as they craft their poems. Here, Singer uses haiku, originally a Japanese form of poetry that focuses on nature in only three lines (generally 5 syllables, 7 syllables, 5 syllables). **Contrast this version of the poem with a look at the poem as if it were written as continuous prose** (*A hawk flies by. A feather lands, tells the grass what it knows about clouds.*). Although those 77 characters could fit into a Tweet, Singer has created an evocative poem by her choice of form. Guide the students in discussing the impact of the words and line breaks in this haiku poem.

5. Follow this with **"Cat Hockey" by Lee Wardlaw** (6th Grade, Week 4, page 35), or selections from *Least Things: Poems about Small Natures* by Jane Yolen or *The Cuckoo's Haiku* by Michael J. Rosen.

FEATHER
by **Marilyn Singer**

A hawk flies by.
A feather lands, tells the grass
what it knows about clouds.

WEEK 7: IN THE WATER

SEVENTH GRADE

Take 5!

1. **Before reading the poem aloud, find an image or video of a shark and display or play it without sound** in the background while you share the poem. A good source for the video is Video.NationalGeographic.com.

2. **Ask eight artistic volunteers to make a quick sketch of what is depicted in each line of the poem** (one volunteer per poem line). Project each sketch, slide-show style, as you reread the poem aloud, line by line. Then display the sketches in a row horizontally, using each line of the poem as a caption for each image.

3. **Invite students to share "fish" stories**—true or exaggerated stories about fishing or beach experiences.

4. Poets arrange their words and lines in a variety of ways to give their poems a certain rhythm. Here, **the poet uses traditional four-line quatrains for each stanza**, but alters the rhythm slightly as a thought crosses two lines (*Keeping his mouth beneath / The surface*). Talk with students about how the poet uses rhyme in this poem, including end rhyme (*beneath/teeth; ocean/motion*), "slant" or "almost" rhyme (*speed/beneath/teeth*), and a combination of slant and internal rhyme in the middle of lines (*swimming/finning*). Then read the poem aloud again.

5. Read about another ocean creature in **"Leafy Sea Dragon" by Steven Withrow** (8th Grade, Week 7, page 193), or compare this poem with "Shark" by Kate Coombs in *Water Sings Blue: Ocean Poems*.

THE POETRY FRIDAY ANTHOLOGY

THE SHARK
by X.J. Kennedy

The shark carves waves with lightning speed,
Keeping his mouth beneath
The surface. When he opens wide
He flashes long sharp teeth.

Should you go swimming where large sharks
Are finning through the ocean,
You might be smart to leap for shore
With haste and not slow motion.

WEEK 8: IN THE AIR

SEVENTH GRADE

Take 5!

1. Another nature-themed poem calls for another video backdrop to set the stage for the reading. **Research a video of a hawk flying and play it without sound** while you read the poem aloud. A good option is this 20-second clip of a red-tailed hawk: http://www.allaboutbirds.org/guide/Red-tailed_Hawk/videos.

2. In a follow-up reading, display the words of the poem and **invite students to choose their favorite line and chime in when that line appears.** You read the first two lines alone, then students join in with you on their preferred lines.

3. For discussion: *If you could be any animal, what would it be?*

4. **Lead a discussion about the experience of reading or listening to this poem in contrast with viewing a digital video adaptation of the poem.** You can find a "poem movie" for this poem on the PFAMS blog (PFAMS.blogspot.com). Contrast what they "see" and "hear" when reading or listening to the poem with what they perceive when they watch the movie based on the poem. Also consider how using video as a backdrop for the initial poem reading compares with watching a video of the entire poem.

5. Revisit **"Feather" by Marilyn Singer** (7th Grade, Week 6, page 115), or follow with selections from *Whose Nest Is This?* by Heidi Bee Roemer.

SPIRAL GLIDE
by **Mary Lee Hahn**

Watching a hawk
soar in a thermal
I become him—
not flapping my wings
just leaning, turning, rising.
Up and up, above,
over, hover.
A dot lost
in the midday haze.

WEEK 9: WEATHER

Take 5!

1. Before reading the poem aloud, **ask students to visualize what a "small tuxedo cat" might look like.** Then read the poem out loud slowly.

2. For a follow-up reading, invite four volunteers to join you. (They can each choose a partner if needed for extra confidence.) **You read the whole poem aloud again, and each volunteer or pair takes one of the lines beginning with *And now*** (lines 9, 10, 11, and 12).

3. **Open the floor to sharing observations of animal behavior from students' own experiences.**

4. Poets enjoy experimenting with writing poetry in different forms and formats. **One very classic form is the sonnet, which has several variations.** Here, it is a 14-line rhyming poem with a distinctive rhythm, ten syllables per line, and a "turn" at the end with a problem solved or a question answered. Talk with students about how the poet uses the elements of this form and identify each component (the number of lines, the rhythm and number of syllables per line, rhyming words, and "turn" at the end).

5. Revisit **"Monday's Cat" by Michael J. Rosen** (7th Grade, Week 5, page 113), or compare this with another poet's observation of her neighborhood scene in "Out My Window" by Amy Ludwig VanDerwater (*The Poetry Friday Anthology K-5 Edition*; 3rd Grade, Week 14, page 160).

AFTER THE BLIZZARD, OUTSIDE MY WINDOW
by Lesléa Newman

The still white street a-glitter in the sun
is traversed by a small tuxedo cat
who tiptoes gently as a solemn nun
then leaps and rolls, a circus acrobat!
His black fur dusted with a coat of snow
he sits to give his left hind leg a lick
'til startled by the cawing of a crow
he looks about him: could this be a trick?
And now the squirrel waves her windblown tail
And now the sparrow sings her morning song
And now my neighbor comes out for his mail
And now the black cat stands and moves along
To think that all of this is mine for free,
The world is so much better than TV!

WEEK 10: FOOD

Take 5!

1. As a fun prop to add interest, **gather any of the foods mentioned in this poem** (tangerine, cherry pie, Havarti cheese, Honeycrisp apple, ketchup) or simply a lunch bag, spoon, or fork. Pile the props in front of you and read the poem aloud.

2. **Share the poem aloud again and invite two volunteers to choose a partner each.** One pair reads the second stanza and one pair reads the third stanza while you read the beginning and ending stanzas aloud. Use the poetry props, too, if available.

3. For discussion: *What are the best and worst parts of lunch at school?*

4. Poets often use vivid language to create imagery. Talk with students about how key words are used in this poem to paint a picture in your mind. **Challenge them to identify words, phrases, and lines in this poem that are particularly descriptive.** Contrast the words and images in the second stanza with those in the third stanza. After this discussion, share the whole poem aloud again.

5. For another ode to freedom to eat, read **"Braces," also by Mary Quattlebaum** (8th Grade, Week 11, page 201) or **"Food Fest" by Heidi Bee Roemer** (8th Grade, Week 10, page 199). In addition, share selections from *First Food Fight This Fall* by Marilyn Singer.

WHAT I WANT TO BE
by Mary Quattlebaum

I want to be
free to eat lunch
whenever I want.

Free to peel
a tangerine
at 7:12 a.m.
or take a spoon
to a whole cherry pie.
Plop down,
at the touch of midnight,
with a hunk
of Havarti
and a sliced Honeycrisp.

No mystery meat
in my happy ever after.
No who-knows sauce
in my dream come true.
No ketchup vats,
saved seats,
chattery forks.
The 12:10 school bell
better not ring

the day I saunter out,
dollars in my pocket,
time loose
on my wrist,
and my smile
hungry
for all the lunch ahead.

WEEK 11: MORE FOOD

Take 5!

1. For a very simple poetry prop, **grab a paper plate and put a large, bold question mark on it**, or cut out a paper question mark and tape it to a plastic plate. Show the plate and read the poem aloud.

2. **For a follow-up reading, invite two volunteers to join you.** (They can each choose a partner if needed for extra confidence.) One volunteer or pair will read the lines attributed to the uncle, reading the italicized words in the first stanza in a deep, commanding voice. The other volunteer or pair will read the narrator's response italicized in the third stanza in a quiet, normal voice. You read the rest of the poem along with them.

3. **Discuss the pros and cons of being a vegetarian versus a carnivore.**

4. Repetition is a key ingredient in creating poems. Sometimes a poet uses repetition not just to enhance the sound of the poem, but to emphasize meaning. **Lead the students in discussing how the poet repeats the phrase "every year"** in this poem to heighten the sense of frustration the narrator feels.

5. Contrast this poem with another poem about uncles and food choices, **"Names" by Julie Larios** (6th Grade, Week 10, page 47), or make a cross-genre connection with nonfiction and a vegetarian cookbook such as *Teen Cuisine: New Vegetarian* by Matthew Locricchio.

SAYING NO
by Amy Ludwig VanDerwater

Have a piece of bacon,
my uncle says
holding a crispy red strip,
sniffing it like fine perfume.
Bacon isn't real meat
so bacon-eating
isn't cheating.

Every year he finds me.
Every year my grandma,
aunts, parents, and cousins
look at me—waiting to see
what The Vegetarian will do.

Every year I smile.
Every year I say, *No thank you.*

Every year my uncle dangles
a fatty bit of pig
in front of my face
laughing
just like those guys
who offer me cigarettes on the bus.

WEEK 12: HOUSE & HOME

Take 5!

1. To set the stage for this poem, **look for photos of abandoned houses to display while reading the poem aloud.** One source is ThisOldHouse.com, particularly the "Before and After" renovation photos of abandoned homes.

2. **Collaborate with students to create a slide show version of this poem.** Research five photos of abandoned houses, one house for each three-line description of the house in the poem. If possible, seek out photos that echo the details in the poem text (e.g., *abandoned; windowpanes broken; porches in shambles; overgrown gardens, scary*, etc.). End with one photo of a renovated home to echo the turn in the final three lines.

3. For discussion: **What makes a house scary?**

4. Poets give their poems shape and structure in many ways. Talk with students about how the **short lines and line breaks give this poem a distinctive rhythm.** The poet uses indenting and rhyme (*bleak/creak; shambles/brambles; disdain/again*) to add emphasis to the description of deteriorating houses. These houses just sound worse and worse as the details pile up, until the end of the poem when the poet turns the tables and suggests no house is beyond hope.

5. Connect to **"Her Room" by Laura Purdie Salas** (8th Grade, Week 12, page 203); selections from *America, My New Home* by Monica Gunning; or *Home: A Collaboration of Thirty Authors & Illustrators*, edited by Michael J. Rosen.

Fixer-Upper
by Terry Webb Harshman

Some houses look scary,
    abandoned
        and bleak,
with windowpanes broken
    and shutters
        that creak,

with lawns unattended,
    and porches
        in shambles,
and overgrown gardens
    of thistles
        and brambles.

But don't look upon them
    with fear
        or disdain;
they just need the love of
    a family
        again.

WEEK 13: FAMILIES

SEVENTH GRADE

Take 5!

1. **Set the stage for this serious, thoughtful poem by displaying a photo of an elderly relative** of your own or from a source like Grandparents-day.com.

2. If possible, **work with one female student volunteer to pre-record her saying "Everything will be all right"** using your cell phone, recording device, or a program like VoiceThread. Then read the poem aloud again, playing that short recording when you get to that line in the poem.

3. For discussion: *Which is harder to accept, change or loss?*

4. **Lead a discussion about the experience of reading or listening to this poem in contrast with viewing a digital video of the poem**, including contrasting what students "see" and "hear" when reading the text to what they perceive when they listen or watch the video. Look for the "poem movie" featuring this poem available on the PFAMS blog (PFAMS.blogspot.com). How does each version of the poem—print version and film version—communicate the mood or tone of the poem?

5. Connect to another poem about family memories, **"Fishing Trip" by Charles Waters** (6th Grade, Week 17, page 61), or selected entries from a verse novel by Jen Bryant, *Kaleidoscope Eyes*.

GRANDMA'S HOUSE
by Kate Coombs

The boxes we packed full of books
are gone now, the chairs
and pictures, the throw rugs,
the china cats, even the dust.

When we walk down the stairs,
my mom takes one more look
around the empty hall,
closes the last window,
touches the bare white wall.
And there by the door
she hugs me hard and tight,
whispering like Grandma did,
"Everything will be all right."

But her voice quivers, and nothing
is the way it used to be
as Mom steps out into the night
and turns the key.

WEEK 14: COMMUNITY

Take 5!

1. Everyone loves a baby picture, so **display a baby photo** of yourself as a baby, of someone in your family as a baby, or from a photographer's website. Then read the poem aloud against this photo backdrop.

2. In a follow-up reading, display the words of the poem and **invite students to choose their favorite two-line couplet and chime in** when that couplet appears.

3. Invite students to share favorite tips for babysitting; refer to resource books like *Don't Sit On the Baby! The Ultimate Guide to Sane, Skilled, and Safe Babysitting* by Halley Bondy. **Talk about how baby sign language can be used to communicate with babies using simple gestures.** See BabySignLanguage.com for tips.

4. Discuss with students that many poems rhyme, but not all. **Guide students in seeing how the poet has given the poem a definite structure.** Sones uses the two-line couplet with space between each couplet stanza to establish the rhythm and pacing of the poem, adding detail after detail, until we get to the surprise ending.

5. Connect to another poem that involves babysitting, **"Cod" by Holly Thompson** (8th Grade, Week 36, page 251), or selections from *One of Those Hideous Books Where the Mother Dies* by Sonya Sones.

SITTING FOR TRISHIE DEVLIN
by **Sonya Sones**

When Trishie
grins up at me,

with those two
little teeth of hers,

and takes hold of my finger
with her tiny pudgy hand,

I can't help thinking
that if I didn't need the money

I'd probably
pay her parents

to *let* me
babysit for her.

WEEK 15: STUFF WE LOVE

SEVENTH GRADE

Take 5!

1. **Gather as many of the objects mentioned in this poem as you can to display as poetry props** (pencil, saw, square, nails, rasp, file, brush). Then read the poem aloud, showing each available object as it is mentioned in the poem.

2. **This time, read the poem aloud backwards**, beginning with the final line, and invite students to chime in on any of the key "tool" words in each line (*hands, brush, file, rasp, nails, square, saw, pencil*). How does the poem change when we read it backwards? Instead of instructions for building, we are revealing the secrets behind the finished product.

3. **Encourage students to talk about things they have made by hand** as part of a hobby or a job or simple crafts created as a young child. Look at the website Etsy.com, a source of handmade arts, crafts, and objects from around the world.

4. **Here the poet uses both rhyme and repetition to create an almost chant-like poem.** Talk with students about the repeated elements (the opening words *I used this/these* and the naming of various tools), about the use of rhyme to connect lines and propel the poem forward, and about the sequencing of lines to suggest a "how to" order for constructing with wood.

5. Revisit **Terry Webb Harshman's "Fixer-Upper"** (7th Grade, Week 12, page 127) or, for another kind of handiwork, read selections from *Eight Hands Round: A Patchwork Alphabet* by Ann Whitford Paul.

THESE HANDS
by **Renée M. LaTulippe**

I used this pencil to plot a design
I used this saw to split the pine
I used this square to angle things right
I used these nails to join boards tight
I used this rasp to curve and scrape
I used this file to smooth and shape
I used this brush to stain the pine
I used these hands to make this mine.

WEEK 16: HOLIDAYS

Take 5!

1. Use whatever materials you have on hand (newspaper, construction paper, string, yarn) to **gift wrap an empty box, and place it in front of you** as you read the poem aloud.

2. Prior to your follow-up reading, **invite students to suggest a simple image for both stanzas of the poem, such as a bridge and a buried hatchet. Sketch each one quickly Pictionary-style in front of the students.** Then read the poem aloud again showing both sketches as you read. Display a copy of the poem alongside these two images.

3. For discussion: *Which is harder, apologizing or forgiving?*

4. Sometimes poets use everyday or colloquial language in their poems for a particular effect. **Work with students to identify the poet's use of idiom**—an expression that is not meant to be taken literally, like "kicked the bucket." Discuss how the idiom *bury the hatchet* is employed in this poem and what it might mean in this context.

5. Follow with another poem using idioms, **"Mom Talk" by Kristy Dempsey** (6th Grade, Week 13, page 53), or develop the theme of forgiveness with Joyce Sidman's *This Is Just to Say: Poems of Apology and Forgiveness*.

SEASON TO FORGIVE
by Ken Slesarik

A gift will often give a lift
and mend the deepest, darkest rift.
It heals the hurt. It soothes the soul.
It builds a bridge that makes us whole.

This season I will seek amends
with former foes (my future friends).
I'll close the door on pain and latch it,
give a gift and bury the hatchet.

Seventh Grade

Week 17: Time Together

Take 5!

1. For an atmospheric backdrop for this poem, project a movie still or movie poster from any "Dracula" movie. One source is IMDB.com. Then **read the poem aloud, altering your voice slightly for each of the two sisters and the anonymous moviegoer**, whose parts are all in quotation marks.

2. Now **invite three students to volunteer to take the parts in dialogue in the poem**: two girls to be the narrator and her sister and one boy or girl to be the anonymous moviegoer. Take a moment to clarify whose line is whose. Then you read the rest of the poem aloud as they chime in on their parts. Make a podcast recording of the reading, too.

3. For discussion: **Why are scary movies so popular if they are so scary?**

4. This is a poem with two main characters. Talk with students about how the reader or listener knows whose point of view is whose in the poem (using quotation marks as a clue) and how **differences in point of view create suspense and humor**. Does the poet use dramatic irony to make a point? (Lisette loves vampire movies though she covers her eyes; the sisters stay to watch the beginning of the movie despite Lisette's fears.)

5. For a film connection, share the poem **"Movies of Us" by Michael J. Rosen** (8th Grade, Week 17, page 213), or for more "monster" poems, read selections from *Vampire Haiku* or *Zombie Haiku* by Ryan Mecum.

The Poetry Friday Anthology

DRACULA
by Carmen T. Bernier-Grand

My sister Lisette loves vampire movies.
We enter the theater
when the movie is a quarter of the way.
When Dracula is about to bite
the pretty lady's neck,
my sister covers her eyes with her hands.
"Tell me when Dracula is gone," she says.
"Shush!" somebody says from the back.
I nudge her with my elbow
when Dracula is gone.
"What happened?" Lisette asks.
"Shh!" says the person in back again.
"Did Dracula bite her neck?"
"No," I say. "She was wearing a cross."
"Shh!"
When the movie ends,
we stay in our seats
to watch the first quarter we missed.

WEEK 18: HUMAN BODY

Take 5!

1. **Before reading this poem aloud, ask a student to indicate how tall a friend or family member is without using words (only gestures).** Then read the poem aloud making the gestures indicated in the poem (hand out, palm down horizontally; then hand out, palm up vertically).

2. For a follow-up reading, stage a "tableau," a frozen moment of the poem posed as a "scene." **Invite four student volunteers to pose as described in the lines of each stanza**: two students for the parts of the "girl" and the poet in the first stanza, and two students for those same parts in the second stanza. Photograph and/or film the tableau and post it with the poem.

3. Sometimes poets weave facts and information into their poems as the poet does here (*corn plants, llamas*). **Do some quick collaborative research on Quito, Ecuador to add to the details provided in the poem.**

4. **Lead a discussion about the experience of reading or listening to this poem in class in contrast with hearing and seeing the poem presented by the poet herself.** Look for the video featuring this poem available on the PFAMS blog (PFAMS.blogspot.com). Discuss what students notice when reading or listening to the poem as performed in class in contrast with what they perceive when they watch the poet share her poem in the video.

5. Revisit a previous poem focused on the importance of hands with **"These Hands" by Renée M. LaTulippe** (7th Grade, Week 15, page 133). Look for poems from around the world in *This Same Sky* by Naomi Shihab Nye and, if time allows, seek out poetry biographies about famous Latinos by Carmen T. Bernier-Grand: *César: ¡Sí, Se Puede! Yes, We Can!*, *Frida Kahlo, Frida: ¡Viva la Vida! Long Live Life!*, and *Diego: Bigger than Life*.

How Tall Is the Boy?
by Joy Acey

Asks a round-faced native girl
    in Quito.
To answer, I put my hand out, palm down
    above my shoulder.
She laughs and
    explains this palm-down gesture
    is used
for animals and inanimate objects—
    corn plants, piles of laundry,
    dogs and llamas.

She tilts my hand up to show how people
    are measured
in her culture, to show respect;
    the hand vertical
    with fingers
reaching toward the sky.

Week 19: More Human Body

Take 5!

1. Before reading the poem, **look for a sample testing or application form.** Post this as a prop while you read the poem aloud.

2. Read the poem again slowly and **invite students to join in on the words in italics** (*what; who*) at the end of the poem for added emphasis.

3. **Talk about the Census demographics in your own community.** Which cultural and ethnic groups are represented? If necessary, use government data available on the web at Census.gov (use the Quick Facts link to find information about your own state, city, or town).

4. Discuss with students that many poems rhyme, but not all. **This poem is an example of** *free verse*. It doesn't rhyme, but guide students in seeing how the poem still has a structure and rhythm based on the line length and line breaks, with short lines offering greater emphasis. Then read the poem aloud again listening for that rhythm.

5. Revisit **"How Tall Is the Boy?" by Joy Acey** (7th Grade, Week 18, page 139) or share excerpts from *The Poet Slave of Cuba*, *Hurricane Dancers*, or *The Lightning Dreamer*, all novels in verse by Margarita Engle.

WHO AM I?
by Margarita Engle

Each time I have to fill out a form
that demands my ethnic origin, I try
to do the math. Half this, half that,
with grandparents who were
probably
half something else, or maybe
a quarter,
or an eighth.

Why do forms always ask
what I am, instead of asking
who?

Week 20: Art & Colors

Seventh Grade

Take 5!

1. **If you have any art supplies or paint handy, place those materials in front of you** as you read the poem aloud.

2. Accompany another reading of this poem with a "tableau"—a frozen moment of the poem posed as a "scene." **Ask for three student volunteers, one for each stanza of the poem, and incorporate the art supplies, if available.** Then read the poem aloud again, moving from actor to actor as you read each stanza.

3. For discussion: *What does a painting of happiness look like?*

4. Some poems are obviously humorous, some are clearly serious, and some are in between. **Talk with students about how this poet uses language to create mood in this poem and how the mood shifts during the course of the poem** (sad in the first and second stanza, then happy in the final stanza). Challenge them to identify words and phrases that convey the mood in each instance.

5. Follow this with another poem about art and colors, **"A Perfect Day" by Julie Larios** (8th Grade, Week 20, page 219), or selections from Jan Greenberg's art-based anthology *Heart to Heart*.

Just Wanted to Tell You
by Patricia Hubbell

The day you moved away
I went to my room
to paint a picture of sorrow,
but the lid to my black paint
was screwed on tight—
not even my pliers could budge it.

I thought about you—
how we played Scrabble for hours,
walked in the rain, talked and talked . . .

A picture of joy leaped into my head.
The lids to my bright paints
fell off in my hand—
happiness floated over my paper.

WEEK 21: LOVE & FRIENDSHIP

Take 5!

1. **Display an image of a smile and an image of a pair of eyes while reading the poem aloud.**

2. Share the poem aloud again and **invite two volunteers to choose a partner each**. Have each pair read one of the last two final lines aloud.

3. For discussion: *Which is more important, a look or a smile?*

4. Talk with students about the structure of this poem and how the poet uses **four-line stanzas (quatrains), the most common form in poetry**, with every two lines rhyming. Lead students in identifying each pair of rhyming words (*book, look; aisle, smile; too, do*).

5. Follow with another poem about budding love, **George Ella Lyon's "How Romantic Can You Get?"** (8th Grade, Week 21, page 221), or selections from *More than Friends: Poems from Him and Her* by Sara Holbrook and Allan Wolf.

LOOK MY WAY
by **Robyn Hood Black**

Come on—just a peek
beyond your science book.
Past that table full of jocks—
Give me just one look?

Look past Mr. Kim
as he patrols the aisle.
Can't I have the quickest flash
of that dazzling smile?

Do you know my name?
I'm in your homeroom, too.
Oh, no—Help! You looked at me . . .
Now what do I do?!

Week 22: A Kinder Place

Seventh Grade

Take 5!

1. Set the stage for this angst-filled poem by **posing by a mirror while you read this poem aloud**. Or use a small hand-held mirror while reading.

2. Create a dramatic interpretation of this poem with two readers. **Ask for two brave volunteers to read the poem together facing each other**—as if mirror images of each other. They can try the whole poem in unison or decide who will read which stanzas independently.

3. **Do some quick collaborative research on the benefits of crying.** For example, *Psychology Today* reports that on average, men cry once a month and women cry five times a month; men usually cry for two to four minutes, compared to about six minutes for women.

4. Talk with students about how the short lines and line breaks give this poem a distinctive rhythm and shape. **Note the placement of the word "unfairly" on a line by itself.** Why might the poet have chosen to single out that word in particular? (It's the most important word in the poem; it explains the reason for the crying, etc.)

5. Follow with **"In Case You're Reading My Journal . . . I'll Summarize" by Betsy Franco** (8th Grade, Week 30, page 239) or with additional poems by Gail Carson Levine from her collection, *Forgive Me, I Meant to Do It: False Apology Poems.*

COMPANY
by Gail Carson Levine

I just got yelled at,
unfairly.
I'm crying, so
I look in the mirror
for sympathy.

My cheeks glow
with sorrow, my eyes
are slick and bloodshot,
my mouth tilts,
stretched tight.

I cry harder.
There's no remedy
for this misery,
but at least
I'm not alone.

Week 23: Exploring

Take 5!

1. **Place a length of rope in front of you as the perfect prop** for this poem about mountain climbing. Then read the poem aloud slowly.

2. **Lead students in researching images to illustrate a PowerPoint slide show presentation of the poem.** Use key words from the poem to guide your selection of pictures (*steel-toed boots; rope fibers groan as they cling; they carry on*), as well as your own interpretation of the scene. Then add the poem text and read the poem aloud as you view the slide show with the students. If possible, record the audio of the poem reading with a timed narration for the slide show and then set it to play automatically as students enter the room, or air it on the school cable channel.

3. For discussion: *What risks are worth taking and what risks are not?*

4. Sometimes poets use exaggeration to add impact to their poems. **This use of figurative language is called hyperbole. Discuss this element with students and identify its use in this poem** (*There is no / such thing as tomorrow*). Why did the poet use hyperbole in this poem in this way? (Perhaps to emphasize the giant ambitions of the climbers and their focus on their immediate goal—how to get up the mountain now.)

5. Follow this with another poem about exploring, **"Dromedary Ferry" by Juanita Havill** (6th Grade, Week 23, page 73), or selections from *Trailblazers: Poems of Exploration* by Bobbi Katz.

THE WORLD ACCORDING TO CLIMBERS
by Irene Latham

They place their trust in a firm
handshake, steel-toed boots

and hats with wide brims.
Rope fibers groan as they cling

like beads of dew on mutton grass.
They don't lament the lack of wing,

only the fact that they can't fly

without them. They forget *why*,
shift their focus to *how*.

They carry on. There is no
such thing as tomorrow.

WEEK 24: SCIENCE & TECHNOLOGY

Take 5!

1. **Read this poem aloud and follow up with a short video demonstrating the basic principles of gears.** Search for "how gears work" on HowStuffWorks.com.

2. Display the words of the poem and **invite students to chime in on one of the six lines that begins with "I" or "I'd"** as you read the rest of the poem aloud.

3. **Collaborate with students to use Glogster.com to create a quick glog**, a digital interactive poster that pulls together images related to key words from the poem in a new, visual representation of the poem's topic. Consider: *gear, teeth, mesh, quick, turn, watch, transmission, winch, fingers.* Then read the poem aloud again and display it alongside the new glog.

4. Poets often use figurative language like personification to build a powerful, descriptive poem. **Guide students in discussing how this poet has given an inanimate object like a gear human qualities**—and challenge them to identify those qualities specifically. Consider the voice of the gear suggested by all those lines beginning with "I," as well as the "advice" the gear offers to the reader.

5. Connect to another poem describing a "mechanical" process with **"5 O'clock Shadow" by Charles Waters** (8th Grade, Week 18, page 215).

Gear
by Michael Salinger

If I were a gear
I'd have teeth but not a toothbrush
I could mesh with other gears
I would turn in ratio
Depending on the size of my neighbor
If they were bigger
I'd be quicker
If they were smaller
I'd spin slower
I'd turn in the opposite direction
Of my partner near
But together as two gears
We'd get the job done
Whether used in a watch
A transmission or a winch
Remember to keep
Your fingers clear
Or else you just might
Get pinched.

WEEK 25: SONG & DANCE

Seventh Grade

Take 5!

1. **Create historical background for reading this poem aloud by researching images of Seneca Village**, a small village founded by free African Americans in Manhattan, New York, in the early 1800s on land that would become Central Park. Display an image while you read the poem aloud. One source is CentralParkNYC.org.

2. **Share this poem again, but coach the students in using American Sign Language (ASL) for the all-important phrase in quotation marks in the last line**. Read the poem aloud again and invite students to use ASL to sign the last phrase *("This is 'MUSIC'!")*. Gesture down with your index finger for "this"; the sign for "music" looks like you are holding a book of hymns with one hand palm up and then sweeping your other hand across and up toward your chest. For helpful visuals, go to Lifeprint.com.

3. Since this poem is written from the point of view of a boy who is deaf, **senses other than hearing are employed in the descriptions in this poem.** How do we know what instrument he is referring to in the last two stanzas of the poem (*big black thing; vibrating wood*)?

4. In this poem, **the poet uses the element of alliteration to repeat the same sound in the beginning of several words for greater emphasis.** Help students locate examples of this (for example, *s* in *sudden, stickball, stopped* or *w* in *walks waving*). Talk about what effect that adds to the sound of the poem and how this might be particularly significant in a poem about hearing and music.

5. Follow this with another historical poem about these boys of Seneca Village, **"Council of Brothers" by Marilyn Nelson** (8th Grade, Week 23, page 225), or with *Sweethearts of Rhythm*, also by Marilyn Nelson.

THE DEAF BOY
Marcus Smith, ca. 1852
by **Marilyn Nelson**

All of a sudden the stickball game just stopped!
Most of the other boys scattered like shards.
My brother James pointed where the ball dropped,
somewhere deep in Professor Hesser's yard.
Moving his lips, James gestured with eyes and hands
that I was to go inside the Professor's fence.

Most of Seneca signals the Professor's mad,
finger-circling. He walks waving his arms.
I searched through his orderly garden's rows and beds,
ignored by robins taking a break from worms.
Perpetually hurrying and efficient bees
zigzagged, and aimless, tippling butterflies.

As I drew near the Professor's open door
every nerve in my body started shivering
as if a breath of January air
had scattered flurries on a clear day in spring.
I placed my hands on the doorframe. Our ball was laid
on top of the big black thing the Professor played.

He swayed, head back, eyes closed. He raised his brows
twiddling the far right side. Then all ten fingers
pounded the far left side as his face scowled.
And I was pulled through ecstasies and angers
by my hands' touch on the vibrating wood.
"This is 'MUSIC'!" I thought. My whole being heard!

WEEK 26: NONSENSE

SEVENTH GRADE

Take 5!

1. After reading this poem aloud with great melodrama and exaggeration, **you may want to discuss with students what "borscht" is**—a soup made of red beets popular in many Eastern European countries and beyond.

2. Read the poem aloud again, and this time **invite students to chime in on one of the rhyming nonsense words of their choice** (*borscht, worscht,* or *forscht*).

3. For a very short poem, this one has several vivid words such as *bog, crimson*, and, of course, *borscht*. **Discuss their meanings** and why the poet might have chosen those particular words (for humorous effect, for color associations, and so on).

4. **The use of "forced" rhyme is a hallmark of many nonsense poems. It refers to imposing rhyme even when you have to change the words to make them rhyme.** Challenge students to identify the forced rhyme. Here the poet makes that obvious and explicit by changing the spelling and pronunciation of the end words, *worse* and *forced*, so they rhyme with *borscht*. This also contrasts with his correct use of end rhyme in *bog* and *fog*.

5. Share another nonsense poem, **"Mere Shadow" by Robert Weinstock** (6th Grade, Week 26, page 79), or selections from *We Go Together!: A Curious Selection of Affectionate Verse*, also by Calef Brown.

In the Bog
by Calef Brown

Lost and alone
in the dreaded bog.
A crimson moon.
Thick red fog.
The air is like borscht.

This poem is the worscht.
The rhymes are forscht.

Seventh Grade

Week 27: World of Words

Take 5!

1. **Hold a dictionary as a prop** while reading this poem aloud. Open it for emphasis as you read, flipping pages for each new stanza as if you're looking things up.

2. **Collaborate with three student volunteers to create a dramatic interpretation of this poem.** (They can each choose a partner if desired.) Each reader chooses one of the three middle stanzas and plans how to read that stanza aloud, perhaps inviting the class to chime in on key letters or words. Then perform the poem aloud together with you reading the first and last stanzas and the volunteers reading the three middle stanzas. Use the dictionary prop, if available.

3. **Talk with students about commonly misspelled words** in the English language such as *already, believable, conscientious, definite, embarrass, interesting, separate*, and *weird*. One source is Merriam-Webster's MySpellIt.com.

4. **Sometimes poets use basic graphic elements to add interest to their poems, like italics and even punctuation: question marks, hyphens, dashes, parentheses, and ellipses—all of which make an appearance in this poem.** Guide students in discussing how these components add to this poem and help show us how to read the poem, forcing us to pause, change intonation, etc.). Then invite your volunteer actors to perform the poem aloud together again.

5. Share **"Meet The Saurus" by Heidi Mordhorst** (6th Grade, Week 28, page 83) or selections from *BookSpeak!: Poems about Books* by Laura Purdie Salas.

BREAKING THE SPELL
by Debbie Levy

I can't spell—I never could.
Though I can drive a nail in wood,
And figure sums much faster than
Some people—even parents—can.
I just can't spell. I know I should.

But how am I supposed to know
That *flavor* has no *e* but *o*
When *braver* is pronounced the same
But takes the *e*—What is this game?

And how am I supposed to win
With such a word as *discipline*?
Why *s* and *c*, to sound out *dis-*?
What's next—start writing *hisc* for *hiss*?

And between *friends*, what is an *i*?
I leave it out (I cannot lie).
You don't need *i* to *bend* or *send*
Why use an *i* to make a *frend*?

So I can't spell—hey, that's just me,
It's not a huge catastrophe....
Did I spell that?
Well, now I'm shocked.
It seems I've got my brain unlocked.

WEEK 28: BOOKS

SEVENTH GRADE

Take 5!

1. If possible, **have a copy of the novel *Charlotte's Web* ready to show after reading the poem aloud.** Wait to reveal the book until students have had a chance to guess at the book being referenced in the poem. Ask a student who has read the book to summarize it briefly for other students who may have never read it.

2. For a second reading of the poem, **ask ten students to volunteer to read the ten question stanzas** of this poem, one stanza per person. (Or five volunteers can read two stanzas each.) Encourage them to choose their favorite stanza question for their reading. Then perform the poem and record it, if possible, to share at an Open House or other parent event.

3. **Make a collective list of students' favorite books from their childhoods.** Encourage students to sign their names at the bottom of the list and share it with a class of students at a nearby elementary school.

4. **It's not unusual for poets to refer to other poems, stories, people, places, or events with the use of allusions in their poetry.** Lead students in discussing each reference to the novel *Charlotte's Web* in this poem. What is each question in the poem alluding to? (For example, in #1, the poet wonders if Charlotte, the spider, and Wilbur, the pig, can truly communicate. In #7, the poet is joking about author E. B. White's name.)

5. Follow this poem with **"My English Teacher" by Lorie Ann Grover** (8th Grade, Week 28, page 235) or a book based on children's book classics, *Spot the Plot: A Book of Book Riddles* by J. Patrick Lewis.

WILBUR ASKS CHARLOTTE TEN QUESTIONS
by Jane Yolen

1. Is interspecies communication
   actually possible—or necessary?

2. Is the barn our world
   or is the world larger than the barn and yard?

3. Do you really spin silk out of your body
   or are you slowly unraveling through time?

4. How did you learn enough human language
   to mount a publicity campaign?

5. What's with the rat anyway?

6. Can food eat food?

7. Is E. B. white? Gray? Pink?

8. Was he truly a Dear Genius?

9. Did you have to die?
   Couldn't you have just rested up for awhile?

10. Where was Pa going with that axe?

WEEK 29: POETRY POEMS

Take 5!

1. **If you have access to any old or antique leather-bound books, bring one to use as a prop for this poem.** (The perfect choice would be an old copy of *One Hundred and One Famous Poems*, of course.) Then read this poem aloud in a conversational voice.

2. For a visual representation of this poem, **invite students to select two or three words each that they think "dance, punch, wail, pirouette, refuse to sit down, shout back, do the splits, and scream bloody murder."** Make a collage of all these words, display it alongside a copy of the poem, and read the poem aloud again.

3. For discussion: *Where is a "wildness of feeling" welcome in your life?*

4. Poets enjoy experimenting with writing poetry in different forms and formats. One distinctive approach is the prose poem. **A prose poem is written in continuous prose but has the heightened imagery, sensory qualities, and/or emotional impact of poetry.** Guide the students in talking about the prose poem form with this example. Challenge students to identify words, phrases, or images that give it an especially poetic quality (for example, *something unlocks in me; wildness of feeling; These words dance and punch*, etc.).

5. Read another poem by **George Ella Lyon, "How Romantic Can You Get?"** (8th Grade, Week 21, page 221), and follow up with an excerpt from George Ella Lyon's *Where I'm From* or Kathi Appelt's book of prose poems, *My Father's Summers*.

SAVED BY THE BOOK
by **George Ella Lyon**

At the supper table one night, Daddy opens ONE HUNDRED AND ONE FAMOUS POEMS and reads I'm not sure what—"Little Boy Blue" or "Renaissance" or Shakespeare—and something unlocks in me because he has revealed a place, in this house, at this table, where the wildness of *feeling* is welcome. The words sound loud out of that little leather volume. The air has not been let out of them, the fire not damped down. These words dance and punch, they wail, they pirouette, they declare themselves and refuse to sit down, they shout back, they do the splits and scream bloody murder. Hallelujah! Poetry has found me!

WEEK 30: RHYME, REPETITION, & RHYTHM

SEVENTH GRADE

Take 5!

1. Use your math skills to **draw two quick circles on the board. Divide one into fourths and one into fifths** and then launch into your oral reading of this poem.

2. Display the words of the poem and **ask for five volunteers to help read the poem aloud, one volunteer for each stanza of the poem.** Stand in a row with each person reading her or his stanza and you reading the final stanza.

3. If it hasn't come up already, talk with students about the faulty math in this poem. There are five references to "fourths of me." **Talk about how "poetic license" lets you break the rules—even the rules of math.**

4. Repetition is a key ingredient in creating poems. **Sometimes a poet uses repetition not just to enhance the sound of the poem, but to emphasize meaning.** Lead the students in discussing how the poet repeats the phrase "One fourth of me" in this poem to heighten the sense of confusion the narrator feels and perhaps for a bit of comic relief.

5. Revisit **"Who Am I?" by Margarita Engle** (7th Grade, Week 19, page 141) or share selections from *Things I Have to Tell You: Poems and Writings by Teenage Girls*, edited by Betsy Franco.

FOURTHS OF ME
by Betsy Franco

One fourth of me
is at the mall
joking with my friends

One fourth of me's
in cyberspace
stalking her or him.

One fourth of me
is in my room
muffling out a scream.

One fourth of me
is on my phone
texting clever things.

One fourth of me
just wants to know
which parts of me are real

so I can add up
to a whole
and trust the way I feel.

Week 31: Different Forms

Seventh Grade

Take 5!

1. What is the perfect poetry prop to share before reading this poem aloud? A mango, of course. **Place the mango in front of you, read the poem aloud, then slice it and share it** with students.

2. Share the poem aloud again and **invite two volunteers to decide how the second line of each couplet will be read by the students.** They can alternate reading the lines themselves, read the lines together, or lead the students in chanting the lines after you read the first line of each couplet.

3. **Survey students about their favorite fresh fruits and quickly graph the results.**

4. **Here the poet tries a somewhat unusual form of poetry, the ghazal (pronounced like "guzzle"), an Arabic lyric poem that incorporates the repetition of the same ending word in each couplet (*heaven*).** Poems usually rhyme at the end of lines, but sometimes they rhyme in the middle too, which is called internal rhyme. Challenge the students to find the internal rhyming words (including slant rhymes) in the lines of this poem (*know/go/mangoes/grow; treat/sweet/seat; none/ton/fun; substitute/fruit/boot; day/say/way; slide/glide; throat/float; real/steal/peel; no/go/no/mangoes*). Then read the poem aloud again.

5. Read another poem about food by **Lesléa Newman, "According to Bread"** (8th Grade, Week 32, page 243), or selections from *Under the Breadfruit Tree* by Monica Gunning or *I Heard It from Alice Zucchini: Poems about the Garden* by Juanita Havill.

MANGOES
by Lesléa Newman

I've got to know before I go,
do mangoes grow in heaven?

Without that treat that tastes so sweet
don't want no seat in heaven.

If there ain't none—at least a ton—
won't be no fun in heaven.

If they substitute another fruit
I'll give the boot to heaven.

A mango a day like the good doctor say
and I'll make my way to heaven.

Will a mango slide through my fingers and glide
down my throat as I float up to heaven?

Now say for real, are there mangoes to steal
and peel on the way up to heaven?

If you say no, Lesléa won't go—
no mangoes isn't heaven!

WEEK 32: METAPHOR & SIMILE

SEVENTH GRADE

Take 5!

1. **Create an atmospheric backdrop for this poem by sharing a video without sound showing a variety of butterflies** in motion. Then read the poem aloud slowly as students watch the video. One excellent source is Video.NationalGeographic.com.

2. **Invite four artistic volunteers to create a quick visual interpretation of each of the four stanzas** reflecting the various stages of poem emergence. Read the poem aloud again, standing by each image as you read each stanza, and then post the poem and art together—if possible, from the ceiling.

3. Here the poet writes about how poems emerge from September to January to April. Next, **talk about what poems might be doing in July and August.**

4. Poets often use metaphors to compare one thing to another to give us a fresh perspective on both things. **Guide the students in identifying the metaphor in this poem.** What two things are being compared (poems and butterflies) and which attributes do they share (*lay still, silent, slowly unfolding, loose into the world*, etc.)? Challenge students to pinpoint words and phrases from the poem to support their observations. Then read the whole poem aloud again.

5. After this poem, share another poem about poetry such as **"In the Word Woods" by April Halprin Wayland** (6th Grade, Week 29, page 85) or **"A Conversation Between Poets" by Jeannine Atkins** (8th Grade, Week 29, page 237) or selections from Georgia Heard's book, *Falling Down the Page: A Book of List Poems*.

ARS POETICA
by Georgia Heard

In September, small poems lay
still and silent inside your hearts.
If you listened carefully,
you might have heard
the quivering of wings.

In January, from the corner
of your eye, you could have spied
a flutter or two—
poems slowly unfolding,
delicate silken wings.

In April, poems began to appear everywhere!
Rainbow wings beating, flapping,
hovering over desks, hanging
from the ceiling, tips of noses, tops of heads.
It was difficult to get any work done!

Now, your butterfly poems
fly free. You fold the memory
into your hearts. Poems—
small butterflies raised, watched,
let loose into the world.

Week 33: Personification

SEVENTH GRADE

Take 5!

1. Before reading this poem, point out to students that many poems are funny, but some are serious—like this one. Then **read this poem aloud beginning with a quiet voice, getting louder in the middle, and then ending again with a quiet voice.**

2. Share the poem again, and this time **ask for two or three volunteers to be "Courage," reading the words in italics (*Okay; Okay; It's going to be okay*)** while you read the rest of the poem. Make a podcast of this poem and share it with any students, friends, or family members who may need an encouraging word.

3. For discussion: *How do we find courage when we are faced with "choice or change"?*

4. **This is a "poem of address" or "apostrophe" poem in which the poet is speaking directly to the subject.** Poems of address can speak even to objects or animals as if they were human. Whom is the narrator addressing (Courage)? Ask the students to find details from this poem that make it a poem of address, such as the use of "you." Then read the poem aloud again.

5. Revisit **"Saying No" by Amy Ludwig VanDerwater** (7th Grade, Week 11, page 125) and follow up with more poems by Sara Holbrook in *Weird? (Me, Too!) Let's Be Friends.*

THE FEAR FACTOR
by Sara Holbrook

I know you.
You.
Courage,
how you ask for what is mine.
How you swell in my chest,
speak up,
straighten my spine,
and whisper in my ear,
Okay, you say.
Okay.
It's going to be okay.
More than
the shoe, the step,
the doorknob turn.
More than a precipice.
A fall.
A burn.
I fear you will abandon me,
evaporate
and not return.
But every time,
when faced with
choice or change
it is your voice that
cuts through clouds of gray.
Okay, you say.
Okay.
It's going to be okay.

WEEK 34: ON THE MOVE

SEVENTH GRADE

Take 5!

1. **Set the stage for this poem by showing a brief driver education video**, particularly one featuring driving on black ice, as mentioned in the poem. One source is Drive-safely.net; look for "Driving Tips for Bad Weather," particularly "Driving on Ice." Then read the poem aloud, pausing between each stanza. Show the video again after reading the poem.

2. **Stage a "tableau" for each stanza, choosing four frozen moments from the poem to create as "scenes," with one or two student volunteers** posing as described in the lines of the poem as you read the poem aloud. They can change their pose for each stanza or if you have four or more volunteers (one per stanza), each volunteer can tap the next one to keep the flow from stanza to stanza. Photograph and/or film the tableau and post it with the poem.

3. **Talk with students about learning to drive.** Do some quick collaborative research on safe driving practices. For a good source, search "Top 10 Safe Driving Tips" on HowStuffWorks.com.

4. In this poem, **the poet uses the element of alliteration to repeat the same sound in the beginning of several words** for greater emphasis. Help students locate examples of alliteration (e.g., *w* in *whirl, winter, wind; s* in *slicked, surface; b* in *black* and *back;* or *t* in *tire, treads*) and talk about the effect on the beginning of the poem, then on the developing tension. Then read the poem aloud again.

5. Follow this poem with **"Texas, Out Driving" by Naomi Shihab Nye** (6th Grade, Week 34, page 95) and more poems about driving from *Behind the Wheel: Poems about Driving* by Janet Wong.

BLACK ICE
by Joseph Bruchac

The whirl of winter wind
slicked the road surface
black and shiny as an otter's back.

The turn of the season's wheel
caught tire treads and heart
at the same time-stopped moment.

I spun, less like a top
than a whirligig beetle,
caromed into the kiss
of guardrail against bumper
rebounded and stopped
just at the edge.

Then the only breath
left held in my chest
was released at last
to spread its wings,
a bird of thanks.

WEEK 35: SUMMER VACATION

SEVENTH GRADE

Take 5!

1. **Create a word cloud or Wordle of the poem text and display it before sharing the poem.** (See the PFAMS blog for a ready-made word cloud version of the poem.) Then read the poem aloud.

2. **Invite two volunteers to choose a partner each.** Have each pair read one of the first two stanzas aloud with quiet voices while you read the third and final stanza.

3. For discussion: *What are the pros and cons of living in more than one place?*

4. Poets give their poems shape and structure in many ways. Read the poem aloud again and pause dramatically before each stanza. **Lead the students in talking about how the first two stanzas are similar and different and how the third stanza echoes the first two in line length and line breaks.** This patterning helps create symmetry and balance in the poem. Now read the poem aloud again.

5. Revisit **"Who Am I?" by Margarita Engle** (7th Grade, Week 19, 141) or share *The Wild Book* or *The Lightning Dreamer*, also by Margarita Engle.

BILINGUAL
by Margarita Engle

Summer
on the island
of my mother's
family

School year
on the continent
of my father's
family

No wonder I feel
like two people—
two minds,
one heart.

WEEK 36: LOOKING FORWARD

Take 5!

1. If possible, **invite a coach to come and read this poem aloud in class with you,** or record a coach reading the poem (or just the coach parts while you read the rest), and share it in class. If a coach is not available, read the poem aloud yourself and use a low, commanding voice for the "coach" lines in italics.

2. For a follow-up reading, play a video of women's soccer as a backdrop for reading this poem aloud. **Invite one volunteer to "be" the coach and read the coach's lines in italics while you read the rest.** For a good video source, search FIFA.com for "Women's World Cup Soccer."

3. **Poll students about their favorite after-school sports and quickly graph the results.**

4. Sometimes poets use basic graphic components to add interest to their poems or to guide the reader. **Lead students in discussing how the poet uses italics (to indicate the coach's lines and point of view) as well as distinctive spacing** to add to the effect of each stanza, the pauses between stanzas, and the poem overall. Then read the poem aloud again.

5. Follow this with another poem about soccer by **Jen Bryant, "Tryouts"** (6th Grade, Week 3, page 33), or selections from *The World's Greatest: Poems* by J. Patrick Lewis.

WORLD CUP
by Jen Bryant

After practice we walk
    to Megan's house, flop
down on her basement couch
    and watch a taped
World Cup game between
    the American and German women.

Coach points out their great plays:
    see how she was patient there
and didn't shoot too soon?
    and their mistakes:
the defender lost her mark
    did you see that?

We all nod, yes, of course, though
    each of us is daydreaming—
as we watch the passes, shots,
    and corner kicks—
of one day running down that field,
    wearing U. S. A. on our backs.

*"Poetry—**the best words** in their best order."*

❧ Samuel Taylor Coleridge ☙

Poems for Eighth Grade

Poetry TEKS for Eighth Grade

(110.20 (b) (4); (8); (15, B, i, ii, iii))

In **grade eight,** we focus on helping students understand:

- the structure and elements of poetry
- making inferences and drawing conclusions about poems
- supporting opinions with evidence from the poem
- how a poet's use of sensory language creates imagery in poetry
- how figurative language such as personification, idioms, and hyperbole contributes to a poem's meaning
- the effects of similes and extended metaphors in more complex poetry
- the importance of graphic elements (e.g., word position) on the meaning of a poem
- how poets use rhyme scheme and meter in distinctive ways
- the relationship between the purpose and characteristics of different poetic forms (e.g., epic poetry, lyric poetry)

Eighth Grade

week 1	School	The Way You Might Judge *by Janet Wong*
week 2	More School	In the School Band *by David L. Harrison*
week 3	Fun & Games	The Run *by Avis Harley*
week 4	Pets	For Bucky *by Naomi Shihab Nye*
week 5	More Pets	Doors of the 24-Hour Emerg. Veterinary Hosp. *by Virginia Euwer Wolff*
week 6	On the Ground	Safe in My Shell *by Ann Whitford Paul*
week 7	In the Water	Leafy Sea Dragon *by Steven Withrow*
week 8	In the Air	Turkey Vulture *by Leslie Bulion*
week 9	Weather	Sunbeam Confesses Its Love of Geometry *by Mary Lee Hahn*
week 10	Food	Food Fest *by Heidi Bee Roemer*
week 11	More Food	Braces *by Mary Quattlebaum*
week 12	House & Home	Her Room *by Laura Purdie Salas*
week 13	Families	The Café *by Guadalupe Garcia McCall*
week 14	Community	Community Service *by Janet Wong*
week 15	Stuff We Love	The Shell *by Deborah Chandra*
week 16	Holidays	Miss Zayd's Oxford Shoes *by Monica Gunning*
week 17	Time Together	Movies of Us *by Michael J. Rosen*
week 18	Human Body	5 O'clock Shadow *by Charles Waters*
week 19	More Human Body	I Had a Nightmare *by April Halprin Wayland*
week 20	Art & Colors	A Perfect Day *by Julie Larios*
week 21	Love & Friendship	How Romantic Can You Get? *by George Ella Lyon*
week 22	A Kinder Place	The Boy *by Guadalupe Garcia McCall*
week 23	Exploring	Council of Brothers *by Marilyn Nelson*
week 24	Science & Tech	Screen Resolution *by Jacqueline Jules*
week 25	Song & Dance	Rhapsody *by Stephanie Hemphill*
week 26	Nonsense	One-Worders *by J. Patrick Lewis*
week 27	World of Words	Editorial Suggestions *by Naomi Shihab Nye*
week 28	Books	My English Teacher *by Lorie Ann Grover*
week 29	Poetry Poems	A Conversation Between Poets *by Jeannine Atkins*
week 30	RR&R	In Case You're Reading My Journal *by Betsy Franco*
week 31	Different Forms	Immortal *by Kristy Dempsey*
week 32	Metaphor & Simile	According to Bread *by Leslèa Newman*
week 33	Personification	Eviscerate *by Michael Salinger*
week 34	On the Move	Restless *by Joyce Sidman*
week 35	Summer Vacation	Body Art *by Marilyn Singer*
week 36	Looking Forward	Cod *by Holly Thompson*

WEEK 1: SCHOOL

EIGHTH GRADE

Take 5!

1. **Set the stage for sharing this poem by holding a poetry prop related to the poem. In this case, hold up a book with an unusual cover**—something intriguing or unusual and unfamiliar to the students, if possible. Then read the poem aloud slowly.

2. **For a follow-up reading of the poem, invite three volunteers to join you.** (They can each choose a partner if needed for extra confidence.) Each volunteer or pair will read one of the question lines (*Which shirt? / Which pants? / Which shoes?*) while you read the rest of the poem aloud.

3. **Invite students to share memories of their very first days of school** in kindergarten or first grade.

4. Sometimes poets use everyday or colloquial language in their poems for a particular effect. **Work with students to identify the poet's use of idiom**—an expression that is not meant to be taken literally (like "kicked the bucket"). Discuss how this idiom ("don't judge a book by its cover") is employed in the poem (in the title, "The Way You Might Judge" and in the lines *The way you might judge / a book by its cover*) and what it might mean in this context. Challenge them to support their opinions with specific words from the poem.

5. Connect this poem with another poem about identity, **"Who Am I?" by Margarita Engle** (7th Grade, Week 19, page 141), or with another poem about the clothes we choose, "Which?" from *A Suitcase of Seaweed*, also by Janet Wong.

THE POETRY FRIDAY ANTHOLOGY

THE WAY YOU MIGHT JUDGE
by Janet Wong

I changed clothes
three times
this morning,
trying to choose.
Which shirt?
Which pants?
Which shoes?

I'm not confused
about
who I am,
but can you blame me
for over-thinking?

The way you might judge
a book by its cover
I just want a chance
to be chosen—
to share my stories
with you.

WEEK 2: MORE SCHOOL EIGHTH GRADE

Take 5!

1. **Prior to reading this poem aloud, work with the band director or music teacher to show a trombone along with the poem.** Or locate an audiotrack of trombone music to play softly in the background while (or after) you read the poem aloud. One source is TromboneExcerpts.org.

2. **Share the poem aloud again and invite four volunteers to choose a partner each. Then each pair reads one of the lines in the repeated refrain** (the refrain appears in the first and last stanzas). The four lines of the refrain are also repeated singly in the second, third, and fourth stanzas: your volunteers can tackle those too, if they want to, while you read the rest of the poem aloud.

3. Poll students on their own musical talents and quickly graph the results. **Which different instruments do students play** (or are they learning to play) either in school or outside of school?

4. Repetition is a key ingredient in creating many poems. Sometimes a poet uses repetition not just to enhance the sound of the poem, but to emphasize meaning (here suggesting the repetition required in practicing a musical instrument, the frustration with not being very proficient, and so on). Lead students in considering how repeating key lines and stanzas helps build a poem and can add to the distinctive rhythm of the lines. **Here, the poet uses the traditional four-line quatrain for each stanza and repeats the first quatrain of the poem in the final stanza to "frame" the poem.** Then read the whole poem aloud again.

5. Follow this with another poem about practice, **"First Practice" by Amy Ludwig VanDerwater** (6th Grade, Week 14, page 55), or share poems from David L. Harrison's collection of memoir poems, *Connecting Dots: Poems*.

IN THE SCHOOL BAND
by David L. Harrison

I play a slide trombone,
My teacher says I'm flat,
I'm not as good as I'd like to be,
But there's nothing to do about that.

I play the slide trombone,
At least I'm not the worst,
I'm one chair up from the guy who's last,
Twenty-five chairs from first.

My teacher says I'm flat,
I sound all right to me,
First chair practices every night.
When does he watch TV?

I'm not as good as I'd like,
A trombone isn't easy,
Even guys I like a lot
Say I make them queasy.

I play a slide trombone,
My teacher says I'm flat,
I'm not as good as I'd like to be,
But there's nothing to do about that.

WEEK 3: FUN & GAMES

EIGHTH GRADE

Take 5!

1. Use a pair of running shoes as the prop for generating interest in this poem. Place them in a prominent spot and then read the poem aloud. **Pause briefly before reading the "poem within a poem"** (*I love the pace of a real fast race.*).

2. **For a follow-up reading, see if two or three runners in the class would be willing to join in and read with you.** They could read the first two-line stanza to set the stage, the final "poem within a poem" lines, or another part of their choosing. Decide on the preferred arrangement and then read the poem aloud together.

3. **Take a quick poll of student exercise preferences (walking, running, yoga, etc.) and graph the results.**

4. Poets enjoy experimenting with writing poetry in different forms and formats. **Here the poet has invented a completely new form called the intravista. In the intravista poem, words within words are arranged downward to make a poem within a poem.** Guide the students in talking about the form with this example. (Note the *I* in *with* in the first line, *love* in *allover*, *the* in *whether*, *pace* in *outpaced*, *of* in *payoff*, *a* in *that*, *real* in *unrealized*, *fast* in *steadfastly*, and *race* in *braces*.) What does the "second" poem within a poem add to the overall poem (emphasis, pacing, theme)? Then read the poem aloud again.

5. Contrast this form with the acrostic form in **Avis Harley's "Future Hoopsters"** (6th Grade, Week 31, page 89), or read poems from one of Avis Harley's books of different poetry forms, *Fly with Poetry* or *Leap into Poetry*.

THE RUN
by Avis Harley

I love to race w**i**th the wind in my face
    and feel that al**love**r runner's "high."
        Whe**the**r
            out**pace**d or in front of the race,
      the pay**off** is worth
        th**at** try.
Strength un**real**ized
      stead**fast**ly flows,
    and b**race**s me for the last-lap close.

I
love
the
pace
of
a
real
fast
race.

Note: The *intravista* is a new poetic form created by Avis Harley, where words within words are arranged downward to make a poem within a poem.

WEEK 4: PETS

EIGHTH GRADE

Take 5!

1. **To set the stage for this quiet, thoughtful poem, post a "lost pet" sign** from your local community or from a source such as Petfinder.com. Then read the poem aloud, pausing briefly after each line in italics (line 10 and line 19).

2. The phrase *he owned* is repeated three times in the poem (and *owned* alone, once) to emphasize the importance of this lost cat and his place in the household. **Invite four volunteers to read one of those lines each (line 1, line 11, the end of line 14, and the final line, line 26)** while you read the rest of the poem aloud.

3. **Invite students to share tips on searching for a new or lost pet.**

4. Discuss with students that many poems rhyme, but not all. **This poem is an example of *free verse*. It doesn't rhyme, but guide students in seeing how the poem still has a rhythm based on how the poet uses line breaks.** Talk with students about how the poet uses short lines, then longer lines, then short lines again for emphasis and tension in the poem. Then read the poem aloud again.

5. Connect to **David L. Harrison's** poem about memories of a favorite pet, **"He Was So Little"** (6th Grade, Week 5, page 37); with Naomi Shihab Nye's poem about lost pets, "So Far," in *What Have You Lost?;* or with selections from *The World According to Dog* by Joyce Sidman.

FOR BUCKY
(WHO VANISHED NOV. 1 WITHOUT A TRACE)
by **Naomi Shihab Nye**

He owned the yard.
Bustle of bamboo,
curled underneath in crackling
nest of leaves,
circle of birdsong,
he would stretch, stand at back
door, wait.
Light rising up so unobtrusively at dawn,
we had one small gray face to depend on.
And let me mention what morning feels like now...
Inside, he owned the hallway,
corner where he paused, where
rub of head against low wall
erased the paint. He owned the orange chair
with threadbare cushion. Knew he could safely
lie on his back for hours, feet straight up.
Liked the sounds of washing machine, printer,
human hum. Liked no other cats or people.
Only us.
Now every single spot where he stood or slept,
curled or watched,
is bare.
Hard to give up
the single sweet friend—face it—
who, for seven years—witness, presence,
owned the air.

WEEK 5: MORE PETS

EIGHTH GRADE

Take 5!

1. **Bring a leash or other dog paraphernalia to display as a poetry prop before reading this poem aloud.** Pause briefly before the final line.

2. **Work with students to create a quick graphic "novel" rendering of the poem with five panels, one for each stanza of the poem.** (Combine the final line with the stanza above it.) Create one quick sketch for each stanza using key words from the stanza as the caption for each panel. Then read the poem aloud again and display it alongside the graphic "novel" version.

3. **For a cross-genre connection, look for the nonfiction book *ER Vets: Life in an Animal Emergency Room* by Donna Jackson,** or research pet first aid on the Internet at sites like HealthyPet.com. Compare excerpts of factual narrative with this poem in terms of approach, information shared, and emotional impact.

4. Poets use line breaks and stanzas to give their poems structure. Talk with students about each stanza and what it adds to the poem—details, emotions, and tension. **Use the images and captions from the student-created graphic "novel" interpretation to pinpoint how the poet builds suspense in the poem**, identifying key words and key scenes. Then read the poem aloud again.

5. Revisit last week's poem, **"For Bucky" by Naomi Shihab Nye** (8th Grade, Week 4, page 187), or read another poem by **Virginia Euwer Wolff, "What She Asked"** (7th Grade, Week 2, page 107).

DOORS OF THE 24-HOUR EMERGENCY VETERINARY HOSPITAL
by **Virginia Euwer Wolff**

Thick leash in a knuckle grip,
he carries the bewildered Akita in,
wild eyes, blood.
Everyone looks up, watching
the drops trail behind a closing door.

Small cats in boxes hush,
we squeeze our posture down,
squint our eyes,
breath held
by the clock.

See the veterinarian come to him,
her head level with his blood-smeared
Green Bay jersey.
This broad barrel of a man
rubs his neck, looks down

at such a small hive of learning
who holds his future in her expensive hands.
He might cry. And then what?
The doctor puts her palm on his huge arm
and invites him to walk with her.
He goes quietly.

Out through another door
march a bandaged Airedale and his radiant boy,
7th grader? 8th grader?
triumphal,
striding out into the day.

We all see the thin line in the air.

WEEK 6: ON THE GROUND

EIGHTH GRADE

Take 5!

1. **Create a visual backdrop for this poem by sharing a video without sound showing a turtle or tortoise in motion.** Then read the poem aloud slowly as students watch and listen. One source is Video.NationalGeographic.com.

2. **Invite two volunteers to join you in a follow-up reading.** (They can each choose a partner if needed for extra confidence.) The students will read the question lines (*What would they think?*, *What would they say?*), choosing who reads which lines and how. Then you read the rest of the poem aloud. Make a podcast of the reading and play it alongside the nature video of the turtle.

3. For discussion: *If you could be any animal, what would you choose?*

4. Poets often use metaphors to compare one thing to another to give us a fresh perspective on both things. **Guide the students in identifying the extended metaphor in this poem** (the entire poem compares one thing to another). What two things are being compared (turtles and people) and which attributes do they share? Then read the poem aloud again.

5. Follow up with **Sara Holbrook's "The Fear Factor"** (7th Grade, Week 33, page 169), or compare to another turtle metaphor poem, "Dad" in *Good Luck Gold* by Janet Wong.

SAFE IN MY SHELL
by Ann Whitford Paul

I am a turtle.
I live in a shell
of my own making,
tucking my head inside,
hoping no one sees
the me that's really me.
What would they think?
What would they say?
Too scared to find out
I stay a turtle
tucked tight
in my shell,
alone.

WEEK 7: IN THE WATER

EIGHTH GRADE

Take 5!

1. **Begin by showing images of leafy sea dragons** to provide background before reading the poem aloud. One source is the Smithsonian at SI.edu.

2. This poem is full of description and vivid language, often in three-line or four-line segments (e.g., *weirder than / a werewolf / on TV*). Display the words of the poem and **invite students to choose their favorite three-line or four-line descriptive passage and chime in when that passage appears** while you read the whole poem aloud again.

3. **Collaborate with students to use Glogster.com to create a quick glog, a digital interactive poster** that pulls together images and key words from the poem in a new, visual representation of the poem's subject (*leafy sea dragon, horse, Martian monster, werewolf, camouflage, seaweed, shrimp, plankton*, etc.). Display the glog alongside a copy of the poem and read the poem aloud again.

4. Poets give their poems shape and structure in many ways. **Talk with students about how the very short lines and line breaks give this very vertical poem a distinctive rhythm.** Say the lines especially slowly, pausing extra-long at the end of each line to emphasize the line breaks and consider why the poet arranged the words and lines in this way. Then read the whole poem aloud again.

5. Refer to another poem about a sea creature, **"The Shark" by X.J. Kennedy** (7th Grade, Week 7, page 117), or read selections from *At the Sea Floor Café: Odd Ocean Critter Poems* by Leslie Bulion.

LEAFY SEA DRAGON
by **Steven Withrow**

Only girls
like magic
horses.
Won't see *me*
playing
with ponies.
But there's this
Martian
monster,
weirder than
a werewolf
on TV,
who can
camouflage
his body,
like floating
globs of
seaweed,
so that
nobody
messes
with him.
I'm no shrimp,
but sometimes
I wish
I could hide
like that,
bobbing
safe under
the surface.
Too bad
he just eats
plankton
and tiny
spineless bits.
It's tough
being
a dragon
without
any teeth.

WEEK 8: IN THE AIR

EIGHTH GRADE

Take 5!

1. For more poetry about another unusual animal, **read this poem aloud, and then do some quick collaborative research** with students on the attributes of turkey vultures.

2. **Investigate audio recordings of sound effects to add in a follow-up reading of this poem.** If possible, look for the animal sounds mentioned in the poem (tweet, cluck, peep, cheep, hiss, grunt). One possible source is SoundCloud.com. Then read the poem aloud again while playing the sounds in the background as they occur in the poem.

3. Next, guide students in noting what information we learn about turkey vultures in this poem. Sometimes poets weave facts into their poems; talk about how writers can share information in many formats, including poems or paragraphs. **Encourage students to seek out related nonfiction works or relevant websites about this creature** and talk about how writers use these two different formats to share information and communicate with an audience. Then read the poem aloud again.

4. As poets consider the impact of language in their poems, they often use words that sound like sounds; this is called *onomatopoeia*. **Encourage students to identify the poetic element of onomatopoeia in this poem.** What are the sound words the poet uses in this poem (*tweet, cluck, peep, cheep, hisses, grunts*) and how do they add to the impact of the poem? Then read this poem aloud again, emphasizing the sound words in particular and using pre-recorded sound effects, if possible.

5. Connect to **"Spiral Glide" by Mary Lee Hahn** (7th Grade, Week 8, page 119) or selections from *Birds of a Feather* by Jane Yolen.

TURKEY VULTURE
by Leslie Bulion

This vulture
stands
on chickeny feet
and doesn't tweet
or cluck
or peep
or cheep.
It hisses and grunts
and hunts
on the fly
gliding
on thermals of air
with its head scaly red
and wrinkly
and bare.
Its keen nose
knows aromas
from way up there
of detectable
delectable
fare
to share,
so things
dead
(or deader)
had better
beware!

WEEK 9: WEATHER

Take 5!

1. **Talk about how sometimes poets combine poetry with another discipline like science or mathematics to push us to consider each from a fresh perspective.** Here, the poet uses language and imagery from geometry to create a poem about love. Then read the poem aloud.

2. **Challenge the students to create five oversized sketches showing each of the math concepts in the poem**: geometry (in general), parallel (shadows), perpendicular (shadows), acute angles (of light), and obtuse angles (of light). Then display the images while you read the poem aloud again.

3. **Talk with students about their favorite and least favorite things about math.**

4. Poets often use figurative language like personification to build a powerful poem. **Guide students in discussing how this poet has given an inanimate object human qualities,** and challenge them to identify those qualities specifically. Beginning with the title of the poem ("Sunbeam Confesses Its Love of Geometry") and continuing with the use of first person (*I*), and phrases like *travel with the pack* and *sneak off on my own*, the poet gives a sunbeam a human voice. Finally, read the poem aloud again.

5. To continue a math and poetry theme, share **"Fourths of Me" by Betsy Franco** (7th Grade, Week 30, page 163) or "Math" and other selections from *Swimming Upstream: Middle School Poems* by Kristine O'Connell George.

SUNBEAM CONFESSES ITS LOVE OF GEOMETRY
by **Mary Lee Hahn**

It's all well and good
to travel with the pack and make
cloud-weary weekenders
lift their grateful pale faces
to the sky,

but sometimes I
like to sneak off on my own
and slant through kitchen windows
so I can cast shadows
through table and chair legs,
demonstrating all I know
about geometry.

The temporary art
of parallel and perpendicular shadows,
of acute and obtuse angles of light,
pleases both
maker
and
beholder.

WEEK 10: FOOD

EIGHTH GRADE

Take 5!

1. To set the stage for this poem, **bring two of the objects mentioned in the poem, preferably two that are compared to one another** such as a carton of milk and an egg, a lemon and a package of sugar, a package of oatmeal and a sandwich, an ear of corn and a potato, or one zucchini and one tomato. Show the objects and read the poem aloud.

2. **Invite two to four volunteers to join you in a follow-up reading.** (They can each choose a partner if needed for extra confidence.) Challenge them to choose whether they want to read one stanza each, or one line of each stanza each, or the first part of a line and the second part of a line each. Then work together to read the poem aloud.

3. **Make a quick list of all the things that are compared in this poem in four columns (e.g., *chef* : *restaurant* :: *teacher* : *school*).** Then brainstorm other things that can be compared and add them to the list.

4. **In creating images and stories in poetry, poets sometimes use analogies to compare things that are NOT alike.** Help students identify the analogies in this poem, using the list you've created together, and discuss why the poet paired these two unlikely things. What makes each pair of opposites parallel? (Possibilities: job, appliance, food, snacks, vegetables, function, and so on.) Then read the poem aloud together again.

5. Compare to another poem celebrating food, **"What I Want to Be" by Mary Quattlebaum** (7th Grade, Week 10, page 123), or some of the haiku food poems in *Yum! Mmmm! Que Rico!: America's Sproutings* by Pat Mora.

Food Fest
by Heidi Bee Roemer

Chef is to restaurant as teacher is to school.
Stove is to hot as fridge is to cool.

Milk is to drink as egg is to eat.
Lemon is to sour as sugar is to sweet.

Oatmeal is to breakfast as sandwich is to lunch.
Soup is to slurp as carrot is to crunch.

Steak is to chew as shakes are to sip.
Cone is to ice cream as chips are to dip.

Ears are to corn as eyes are to potatoes.
Green is to zucchini as red is to tomatoes.

Fuel is to car as food is to tummy.
Liver is to yucky as pizza is to yummy!

WEEK 11: MORE FOOD — EIGHTH GRADE

Take 5!

1. Did you wear braces when you were younger? If so, **share a photo of you with your braces. Or if you have a friend or colleague who had braces, ask them if they'd be willing to share.** Then read this poem aloud with the photo as your backdrop. You may need to explain words like *kibosh* (stop/end) or *nosh* (snack/eat).

2. **Invite three volunteers to join you in reading the poem aloud again.** (They can invite a partner to join them, if they prefer.) Give them the parts that begin with "O" in lines 13, 14, and 15 (one line each: *O, thick, bright / carrots!; O, popcorn!; O, jagged, salty chips!*). Work with them to coordinate these lines and decide who says what. Then read the poem aloud together.

3. For discussion: **What are the pros and cons of wearing braces?**

4. This is a "poem of address" or "apostrophe" poem in which the poet is speaking directly to the subject. Poems of address can speak even to objects or animals as if they were human. **Ask the students to find details from this poem that make it a poem of address, such as the use of "you" and** phrases like *you / bungle my floppy / tongue* and *tighten me / in your twisted, / oh-so-pricey grip*. Then share the poem aloud again.

5. Revisit last week's food-themed poem, **"Food Fest" by Heidi Bee Roemer** (8th Grade, Week 10, page 199), or read selections from *Food Fight: Poets Join the Fight against Hunger with Poems about Their Favorite Foods,* collected by Michael J. Rosen.

BRACES
by Mary Quattlebaum

Mouth harness.
Tooth binder.
All day you
bungle my floppy
tongue, scatter spit,
tighten me
in your twisted,
oh-so-pricey grip.

But deep in sleep,
I slip your silver bit

and grind my way down
the list of forbidden
treats—O, thick, bright
carrots! O, popcorn!
O, jagged, salty chips!
See my grin, unfixed?
Kiss off, braces.
No more kibosh.

In my dreams,
I freely nosh.

WEEK 12: HOUSE & HOME

EIGHTH GRADE

Take 5!

1. **Before sharing this poem, show the article "The Listening Post" by David Backes from the *Minnesota Conservation Volunteer Magazine*,** available online here: https://webapps8.dnr.state.mn.us/volunteer_index (search by the author's last name). Then read the poem aloud in a quiet voice, pausing briefly between each stanza.

2. **Invite two students to join you in reading the poem aloud again.** (They can each choose a partner if needed for extra confidence.) One student or pair can read the pivotal line found in the second stanza while the other reads the thematic conclusion in the final stanza. Let them decide who reads which, and you read the rest of the poem aloud.

3. **Talk with students about their favorite things about their rooms or homes.**

4. Poets enjoy experimenting with writing poetry in different forms and formats. One modern approach that is gaining momentum is the "found" poem. A found poem is built upon the words from another source, usually text from a non-poetic source like a newspaper or magazine article. **Guide students in talking about the process of creating found poetry from key words taken from another source.** Look for the words in this poem from within the magazine article. (Note that they are found helter skelter throughout the article and not in the same order as in the poem). Point out how the poet has captured a sense of place in her poem that echoes a strong sense of place in the article. Then read the poem aloud again.

5. Connect to a poem about found poems, **"In the Word Woods" by April Halprin Wayland** (6th Grade, Week 29, page 85), or to Georgia Heard's anthology of found poems, *The Arrow Finds Its Mark*.

HER ROOM
by Laura Purdie Salas

Her room,
tucked among
a life turning
busier and more stressful,
wasn't wild.

That was the point.

Rejections were taken
apart and hauled away.

Silence and ideas,
old familiar friends,
became a home.

WEEK 13: FAMILIES — EIGHTH GRADE

Take 5!

1. Before reading this poem, point out to students that many poems are funny, but some are quiet and thoughtful—like this one. Then **read the poem aloud, pausing briefly between each stanza.**

2. **Stage a "tableau," a frozen moment of the poem posed as a "scene," with student volunteers posing as described in the lines of the poem.** One volunteer can pose as Papi at the Café, and multiple volunteers can pose as the narrator on the sidelines—at the barn, at the café, and at home, indicating each place with a simple sign or prop (picture of a horse, sign for the café, a form needing a signature). Read the poem aloud, moving from actor to actor or scene to scene. Photograph and/or film the tableau and post it with the poem.

3. In this poem the poet uses two Spanish words in the first stanza: *su tesoro*. **Talk with students about what the words mean based on context, or look them up: *his treasure*.** Discuss why the poet might have chosen to include them in Spanish (for emphasis, for the sound of the words, to emphasize his culture, etc.).

4. **Here the poet invites us to make our own inferences about what the two major characters in the poem are feeling and experiencing.** What is the father's emotional state? (Happy with his horse, missing his wife, distant from his child.) What is the narrator's emotional state? (Envious of the horse, missing her father's presence, angry with her father.) Discuss with students and challenge them to support their opinions with specific words and lines from the poem. Then read the poem aloud again.

5. Follow this poem with **"Grandma's House" by Kate Coombs** (7th Grade, Week 13, page 129), or read selections from Guadalupe Garcia McCall's books *Under the Mesquite* or *Summer of the Mariposas*.

The Café
by Guadalupe Garcia McCall

Papi went out
And bought himself
A horse last month. He keeps it
In a barn on the outskirts of
Town. It is **su tesoro,**
His dawn of night,
His morning star.

Every day, after
Conversing with his
Horse, he goes to drink coffee
At the local truck stop,
The Café.

Most days, he has
Breakfast there—only

Sometimes does he come home,
Expecting me to cook for him
Now that Mami is gone.

If we need anything,
A signature on a field trip
Form, money for a new pair of shoes,
A ride to school, even food,
We go looking for him
At The Café.

He is a regular there,
As permanent as our loss.

WEEK 14: COMMUNITY

EIGHTH GRADE

Take 5!

1. If possible, **bring the ingredients for making a sandwich**: bread, mayonnaise, ham slices, cheese slices, and lettuce, as well as a knife and a sandwich bag or plastic wrap. Assemble a sandwich and then read the poem aloud.

2. **Invite six students to join you in performing the poem.** They can assemble a sandwich as described in the poem with each student taking one of the steps (bread, mayo, ham, cheese, lettuce, and the wrapping), or they can simply read the lines describing each step (as Max, the narrator, Joe, Julie, Stephanie, and Nick) while you read the rest of the poem aloud.

3. **Do some quick collaborative research on local community service opportunities** for young people, including any experiences students have already had. Post the list for future reference.

4. Point out that sometimes poets borrow the patterns from other things like lists or "how to" directions to create a new poem. Talk with students about how the lines and line breaks give this poem a distinctive rhythm, particularly in the description of the sandwich-making process (with the use of proper names and the repetition of the ending word *and*). Then in the final lines, the poem takes an ironic turn. **Guide students in discussing the irony in helping to make 300 sandwiches and then going home *stomach-growling starving*.** (Are they truly *starving*?) Then read the poem aloud again.

5. Follow this poem with another poem about "work," **"Sitting for Trishie Devlin" by Sonya Sones** (7th Grade, Week 14, page 131), or with a picture book about homelessness, *A Shelter in Our Car* by Monica Gunning.

COMMUNITY SERVICE
by Janet Wong

I thought I'd be crying my eyes out
chopping up onions but
thank goodness the soup kitchen
is serving sandwiches today.
It's an assembly line:
Max takes two slices of bread and
passes them to me,
I slap some mayo on and
pass them to Joe,
Joe peels off three slices of ham,
Julie does cheese,
Stephanie is lettuce and
Nick wraps it up.
Two hours and 300 sandwiches done
we hop on the bus and head back,
stomach-growling starving and
ready to raid our refrigerators
at home.

WEEK 15: STUFF WE LOVE

EIGHTH GRADE

Take 5!

1. **Before reading the poem aloud, display an image of a seashell** such as a conch or a nautilus in the background. One source is Photography.NationalGeographic.com. Then read the poem aloud slowly, enunciating each word.

2. Work with students to find and record simple sound effects to use as a background for another poem reading. This could include the ambient noise of soft voices, the sea, a whirlpool, booming voices, bellowing voices, and a sigh, with two or three students researching and recording each one. One excellent source is SoundCloud.com. **Then read the poem aloud with students providing each sound effect as it fits the poem.**

3. **Talk with students about what they know about seashells,** including names, types, facts, or myths. One source is HowStuffWorks.com (search "Why can you hear the ocean when holding a seashell to your ear?").

4. In this poem, **the poet uses the element of alliteration to repeat the same sound in the stressed syllables of several words in succession** for greater emphasis. Help students locate examples of this (such as *s* in *sea-change, sounds, slide* or *b* in *boom, bellow*). Talk about how this adds to the impact of both the sound and meaning of the poem. Then read the poem aloud again.

5. Revisit **"Safe in My Shell" by Ann Whitford Paul** (8th Grade, Week 6, page 191), or share poems from one of Deborah Chandra's books, *Rich Lizard* or *Balloons*.

THE SHELL
by Deborah Chandra

Sunk
in the warm
sounds
of this room,
the shell hears our voices
lap the glassy edge
of its earlobe . . .

and in a sea-change
of sounds
slide a whirlpool
of roars
down
the whorl
of its ear.

The shell hears
our voices
boom, bellow,
plunge
under—
even your sigh
fills its tunnel
with
thunder.

WEEK 16: HOLIDAYS

EIGHTH GRADE

Take 5!

1. Do you have a pair of oxford shoes (leather lace-up shoes)? If so, bring and display them before reading the poem aloud. If not, **seek and share an image from any popular shoe store website**, like Zappos.com.

2. **Since this poem has a regular rhythm and rhyme, it could be performed as a rap.** See if a student or two might be willing to give it a try. If not, download the inexpensive app AutoRap and try rapping the poem this way.

3. **Inventory the shoes students are wearing today and graph the results.**

4. Poets use rhyme scheme and meter in distinctive ways in creating poetry. Here the poet uses the traditional four-line quatrain form for each of the four stanzas. **Lead students in identifying the rhyme scheme (ABCB) and rhyming words in this poem** (*today/play; shoes/do; new/shoes; pride/provide*). Talk about how the poet uses "slant" or "almost" rhyme for each end rhyme (since each pair is not the same syllable length nor do they rhyme perfectly). Then read the poem aloud again.

5. Follow this with another poem about performing, **"Opening Night" by Renée M. LaTulippe** (6th Grade, Week 25, page 77), or with excerpts from *Bronx Masquerade* by Nikki Grimes.

MISS ZAYD'S OXFORD SHOES
by Monica Gunning

The Christmas season glistened bright.
My mood, a gloomy one today.
My only shoes beyond repair
And I was the reader for our play.

The village cobbler knew me well.
He often had to fix my shoes.
When I told my shoeless tale
I knew he'd think of what to do.

He walked away to his storeroom,
Returned with oxfords, almost new.
"Try these on, me child," he said.
"In heaven, Miss Zayd won't need these shoes."

A little large, but laced up tight.
I could walk on that stage with pride.
The cobbler, my Santa Claus this year.
In his own way, God will provide.

WEEK 17: TIME TOGETHER EIGHTH GRADE

Take 5!

1. **If you have any video footage of yourself as a child or of your family that you would feel comfortable sharing, play a snippet** to set the stage before reading this poem aloud.

2. **For a follow-up reading, invite three or four students to join you in reading the poem aloud.** Two or three students can read the fourth stanza in which the narrator wonders "what if." They can choose whether to read the entire stanza together or divide the lines among themselves. A fourth student can read the final lines in quotation marks attributed to "Dad" while you read the rest of the poem aloud.

3. For discussion: *What are the best and worst things about having younger siblings?*

4. Some poems are obviously humorous, some are clearly serious, and some are in between. Talk with students about how this poet uses language to suggest the tone of this poem. How would you describe the tone of this particular poem? **Is the narrator poking fun at his little brother and the rest of his family? Is he envious of him? Or is he embarrassed by the final comment by his dad?** Challenge students to draw their own conclusions and to support them with lines or passages from the poem. Then read the poem aloud again.

5. Share another poem about movies, **"Dracula" by Carmen T. Bernier-Grand** (7th Grade, Week 17, page 137), or share another poem about younger siblings, **"Giving" by Jane Yolen** (6th Grade, Week 15, page 57).

THE POETRY FRIDAY ANTHOLOGY

MOVIES OF US
by Michael J. Rosen

My brother likes to ride his rocking horse
alongside the cowboys on TV.
Mom can usually zoom through the channels
to find a western so baby-buckaroo
can bounce and bobble and squeal, "giddy-up!"

At first, our Dad grabbed his camera and shot
my brother galloping beside the screen.
Then he replayed those movies for everyone.
Now my brother's favorite thing is watching
himself on TV and squealing even more

as he jumps on his horse and rocks beside
the movie where *he's* the famous cowboy star.
Now Dad thought *that* was the cutest thing ever!
He just had to record my brother riding—live!
and alongside his own cowboy channel.

What would happen if Dad kept playing his latest
movie on the screen and kept recording
my brother watching and riding, again and again . . .
until dozens of tinier cowboy brothers
stampede across the frontier of what comes next?

"Not so fast, big brother," Dad says.
"You want to see our movies of *you* at three?"

WEEK 18: HUMAN BODY

EIGHTH GRADE

Take 5!

1. **It's time for a shaving demonstration!** Bring a razor with the safety guard still on and do a mock demo of shaving your face, even if you're a woman. Or for a video example, go to Howcast.com (http://www.howcast.com/videos/276-How-to-Shave-Your-Face). Then read the poem aloud.

2. **For a follow-up reading, invite the boys to choose their favorite line and chime in** as you read the whole poem aloud again. Use the how-to video as a backdrop (without the sound).

3. Sometimes poets weave facts and how-to steps into their poems. **Guide students in noting what we learn about shaving in this poem.**

4. Lead a discussion about the experience of reading or listening to this poem (when you read it aloud) in contrast with viewing a digital video of the poet reading the poem himself. **Look for the video featuring this poem available on the PFAMS blog (PFAMS.blogspot.com).** What is distinctive about each experience? What is similar? Then read the poem aloud together again.

5. Connect with another shadow poem, **"Mere Shadow" by Robert Weinstock** (6th Grade, Week 26, page 79), or with more coming of age poems in *You Hear Me?: Poems and Writing by Teenage Boys*, edited by Betsy Franco.

5 O'CLOCK SHADOW
by Charles Waters

I dispense shaving
Cream from the metal can.
Looks like I'm holding
A cloud in my palm.
I lather the bottom half of my face,
Take a razor, and begin this experiment.
Up, down, up, down,
Cheeks, chin, upper lip, neck.
Any nicks? (Let me check.)
Remembering to
NEVER go side to side.
"Easiest way to cut yourself,"
Dad told me more than once.
Done, finished.
My chest heaves in relief.
No lie, I am the Man!

WEEK 19: MORE HUMAN BODY

EIGHTH GRADE

Take 5!

1. If possible, **work with the orchestra teacher to bring a violin as a poetry prop.** Or if not available, search for a quick image of a violin to project while you read the poem aloud.

2. **Make a speech balloon sign with &#$* on it. How is that spoken?** Ampersand, number sign, dollar sign, asterisk—which is fun to say on its own. Invite students to join in on saying this "exclamation" when it occurs (twice) in the poem, as well as on the final line of the poem, which reveals the twist, while you read the rest of the poem aloud.

3. **Nearly everyone has had a bad dream about school. Share your own and invite students to talk about a few of theirs.**

4. **Poets can use line breaks to give their poems structure.** Here the poet gives us a list of woes, things that are going wrong, one after another. Talk with students about what each detail adds to the poem (about the violin, about the dog, about cursing, about the audience), building suspense and tension until the final twist in the end line. Then read the poem aloud again.

5. Connect with **"Opening Night" by Renée M. LaTulippe** (6th Grade, Week 25, page 77) or selections from April Halprin Wayland's novel in poems, *Girl Coming In for a Landing*.

I HAD A NIGHTMARE
by **April Halprin Wayland**

I was pulled onto an old, wooden
school auditorium stage.
They wanted me to play my violin for them.
My bow wouldn't tighten.
I forgot which string on which to begin.
I didn't know which key.
I forgot how long to hold the first note.
Then I realized that the neck of my fiddle
was broken
held together by the four strings,
G, D, A, E.
My dog was there
and he ran off
and he wouldn't come when I called
and I said &#$* on stage
and then I realized
they were teachers in the audience—
teachers, students and parents—
and I apologized—
apologized into the microphone
for saying &#$*
and I was thinking:
it's a good thing this is a dream.

WEEK 20: ART & COLORS

EIGHTH GRADE

Take 5!

1. **Before reading this poem aloud, show a color wheel or color grid** with all the primary and secondary colors presented. If you need help, look for Pantone.com, the world authority on color.

2. Work with students to identify all the color words in the poem (*yellow, blue, green, purples, white, brown, red*). Then **invite them to chime in on the color word of their choice** as you read the poem aloud again.

3. **Poll the students about their favorite colors. Make a quick color wheel graph of the results.**

4. Poets often use sensory language to create imagery. Talk with students about how key words are used in this poem to paint a picture in your mind, particularly the color words. **Challenge students to identify words, phrases, or images that evoke the senses**, particularly visual and auditory. After this discussion, share the whole poem aloud again.

5. Connect with another poem about about biking with a friend with **"Biking Along White Rim Road" by Irene Latham** (7th Grade, Week 3, page 109), or follow up with poems about color in *Yellow Elephant: A Bright Bestiary,* also by Julie Larios, or from *Red Sings from Treetops* by Joyce Sidman.

A Perfect Day
by Julie Larios

The sun, limned yellow,
the sky a bayou blue—
those two are best friends forever.
Together they put a green sheen
on the grass. Here we are,
you, me, in the middle
of a perfect day that purples us
to pieces and makes us laugh.
We're riding fat-tired bikes
down a dirt road under white clouds,
when we suddenly pass two
brown cows standing dead still
on a sun-burned hill—we stop
pedaling when the biggest cow's
sudden moo, dark and unexpected,
unglues the smaller cow, not to mention
you, and me, and the perfect day.
How can one cow's call
make us all—even those
tight little thistle heads
trembling in the ditch—
bloom red?

WEEK 21: LOVE & FRIENDSHIP

EIGHTH GRADE

Take 5!

1. **Place a can or bottle of Dr. Pepper in front of you and then read the poem aloud.** If not available, show a clock face with 6:00 on it instead.

2. **For a follow-up reading, invite a boy and a girl volunteer to join you in reading the poem aloud.** (They can each choose a partner if needed for extra confidence.) The boy(s) will read the lines attributed to the boy, Barrett, enclosed in quotation marks (in lines 5, 6, 7, 8) and the girl(s) will read the word "Okay" attributed to the girl, Emmy, in the poem (in line 9). Alert your volunteers to the fact that their words may be embedded within a line. Then you read the rest of the poem aloud.

3. **Lead students in talking about fun things to do for free or low cost.**

4. **This poem is an example of a narrative poem in free verse—a poem that tells a story in unrhymed lines.** Guide students in seeing how the poet uses characters and actions and even dialogue to build a story within the poem. Can you picture the scene? How does each line of the poem advance the story? After you discuss these questions, read the poem aloud again.

5. Connect to a prose poem by **George Ella Lyon, "Saved by the Book"** (7th Grade, Week 29, page 161), or selections from *More than Friends: Poems from Him and Her* by Sara Holbrook and Allan Wolf.

HOW ROMANTIC CAN YOU GET?
by George Ella Lyon

Emmy couldn't go to Barrett's house. His mother
didn't allow visitors. They couldn't go *out-*
out because Barrett didn't have any money
or a car either, never mind that there was hardly
anywhere to go. So he said, "I'll tell you what.
You meet me in the middle of the swinging bridge
at the end of Somerland Avenue at 6 o'clock
and we'll have dinner." (The bridge led across
the river to his house.) "Okay," Emmy said, picturing
peanut butter sandwiches in a paper sack. Huh!

Barrett was nothing if not a magician, from glittery
eyes to gleeful feet, and there in the middle of that
cable-strung path of splintery boards, he produced
two plates of spaghetti (red-sauced and parmesan-
sprinkled), two slices of garlic bread, and a Dr. Pepper
which they split. His idea of romance. Hers too.

Week 22: A Kinder Place

Take 5!

1. **To set the stage for this poem, show images of famous couples in history such as Romeo and Juliet.** These could be from book covers (from Amazon or other sources) or famous paintings (one source: AllPosters.com). Then read the poem aloud, pausing briefly between stanzas.

2. **Collaborate with students to create a quick graphic "novel" rendering of the poem with four panels, one for each stanza of the poem.** Create one quick sketch for each stanza using key words from the stanza as speech bubbles and/or captions for each panel. Then read the poem aloud again and display the poem alongside the graphic "novel" version.

3. **Discuss with students what they guess might happen to the poem's characters AFTER the end of the poem.** Challenge them to support their conclusions with details from the poem.

4. Poets use similes to compare one thing to another to give us a fresh perspective on both things. **Lead the students in identifying the similes in this poem** (*like the soft feathers; like the sunset*). Discuss the things that are being compared to one another (shoulders and feathers; eyes and sunset) and the impact the similes have in the poem. Then share the poem aloud again.

5. Contrast this poem with the romantic experience in **"How Romantic Can You Get?" by George Ella Lyon** (8th Grade, Week 21, page 221), or with excerpts from the novel in verse *What My Girlfriend Doesn't Know* by Sonya Sones.

THE BOY
by Guadalupe Garcia McCall

There is a boy in my Economics
Class who says he knows me.
He has dark, blonde hair that falls
To his shoulders like the soft feathers
Of an ***aguila***. His eyes are amber
Lights that sparkle like the sunset.

He likes to tease me, and even
Says he gave me ***empanadas*** once,
Back when we were small. I look
Down at the floor and say I don't
Remember. But in his eyes I see
The embers of a thousand burning
Fires. He smiles at me every day
And has even changed seats to sit
Beside me. Myrtala teases me
And says, "Maybe he likes you."

Today, he showed up at my house.
He drove up in his truck, got out,
And smiled as he clung to the chain
Link gate and called out my name shyly.

My father went outside to ask him
What he wanted. Papi told him there
Was nothing here for him, told the boy
I am not allowed to date, made him
Turn around, get back in his truck,
And drive off into the sunset.

WEEK 23: EXPLORING   EIGHTH GRADE

Take 5!

1. **Before sharing this poem, show images of the California Gold Rush to build an understanding of the background.** One source is The Virtual Museum of the City of San Francisco (SFMuseum.org); select "1849 California Gold Rush." Then read the poem aloud slowly.

2. For a follow-up reading, **invite any students who want to volunteer to shout out the newspaper headline in line 13** while you read the rest of the poem aloud.

3. Sometimes poets weave facts into their poems. Guide students in noting what information we learn about life in 1849 from this poem. **Talk about how writers can share information in many formats, including poems or paragraphs.** Do some quick collaborative research on the Gold Rush together using print or online sources.

4. **Poets enjoy experimenting with writing poetry in different forms and formats. One very classic form is the sonnet, which has several variations.** This particular example is a nonce sonnet, a 14-line poem with no set rhyming pattern, but with a distinctive rhythm and a "turn" at the end with a problem solved or a question answered. Talk with students about how the poet uses the elements of this form and identify each component (the number of lines, rhyming words, and "turn" at the end). Then share the poem aloud again.

5. Share another poem by **Marilyn Nelson, "The Deaf Boy"** (7th Grade, Week 25, page 153), or selections from her book *Carver: A Life in Poems*.

COUNCIL OF BROTHERS
*James, John, Michael, Hugh, and Patrick Donnelly,
January, 1849*
by **Marilyn Nelson**

Our Mam, dead of fever, sleeps on the ocean floor.
Now cholera's took Dad. Listen to me:
All of our lives, we've been hungry and poor.
Well, I've had it up to here with poverty!
Laying awake every night with a growling gut,
wearing Hugh's smelly, outgrown, leaky boots.

Jamie's free, white, and almost twenty-one;
all of us have strong hearts and arms and backs;
I'm thirteen, but I'm strong as any man.
We are the orphans of the dispossessed.
What's to keep us from being rolling stones?

This morning, I hawked a headline hot off the press:
EXTRA! GOLD FOUND IN CALIFORNIA CREEK!
I say the Donnelly brothers should head West.

WEEK 24: SCIENCE & TECHNOLOGY   EIGHTH GRADE

Take 5!

1. **Turn the text of this poem into a word cloud or Wordle** and display the graphic to set the stage for this poem about technology. Then read the poem aloud slowly.

2. Now **invite students to chime in on one of the last two lines**—their choice—while you read the rest of the poem aloud again.

3. Images can look different to different people depending on how they are presented or how we see them. **Use images from Illusions.org to talk about how perception can trump truth** in how we understand what we see.

4. Here the poet expects us to be familiar with the jargon of technology. **Work with students to identify the key vocabulary words that are essential to understanding the poem (e.g., *HTML, browser, pixel resolution*, etc.).** What point is the poet trying to make about technology? Discuss with students how the poet also uses technology as a metaphor for how we each see things differently. Challenge them to support their opinions with specific words from the poem. Then read the poem aloud again.

5. Follow with another poem about technology, **"Silence" by Linda Kulp** (6th Grade, Week 24, page 75), or selections from *Technically, It's Not My Fault* by John Grandits.

SCREEN RESOLUTION
by Jacqueline Jules

Both dabblers and designers
know HTML is tricky.

Websites skew
depending on the browser,
screen size, settings . . .
Check laptops,
desktops, smart phones, tablets. . .
you'll see—
a single sentence
neatly placed beneath an image
breaks oddly on another screen.
Nothing looks the same
to the guy who likes his text smaller,
his pixel resolution lower. Vice versa.

No one sees exactly what you see.
A truth older than technology.

WEEK 25: SONG & DANCE

EIGHTH GRADE

Take 5!

1. **Before you read this poem aloud, put on a set of earphones or earbuds as your poetry prop**.

2. Play a Gershwin song before reading the poem aloud again. If possible, **challenge students to find an audiotrack for "I Got Rhythm," the classic jazz standard written by George and Ira Gershwin** and referenced in the poem. One possible source is ListeningLab.Stantons.com.

3. **Collaborate with students to create a playlist** of their top ten current favorite songs.

4. It's not unusual for poets to refer to other poems, stories, people, places, or events with the use of allusions in their poetry. **Lead students in finding and discussing the reference to the music of George Gershwin in this poem.** Clues include: 1924 (the year his landmark "Rhapsody in Blue" was composed) and the lines *I got music / and rhythm* (from "I Got Rhythm"). Then play the music again and read the poem aloud again.

5. Revisit **"In the School Band" by David L. Harrison** (8th Grade, Week 2, page 183), or read excerpts from the novel in verse *Things Left Unsaid* by Stephanie Hemphill.

Rhapsody
by Stephanie Hemphill

The clarinet rests
quietly in its case
as we bump along on the bus.
I block out the noise
and hear the deep
grooves of Gershwin
of his 1924 train
whistling down the track.
There are jeers and jabs
but I sit oblivious
caught up in a riff
of laud and lament
and most of all exultation.
I want to lick my reed,
not open my jaw
to crow and caw
out of step.
I got music
and rhythm
and reverie.

WEEK 26: NONSENSE

EIGHTH GRADE

Take 5!

1. **Set the stage for this unusual word puzzle poem by writing a math formula on the board: x + y = z.** Then read the poem aloud very slowly with a long pause after each word in column one.

2. First, students may want to talk about how the word in column 2 fits the prompt in column 1. Then **invite two or more volunteers to decide how they would like to read this poem aloud**—as a call and response with two people or groups taking each column (or in some other arrangement). Then perform the poem together.

3. **Brainstorm more examples of "one-worders" in two columns** as Lewis demonstrates in his poem. You may want to start "backwards"—thinking of clever word puns and then deciding how to lead up to that answer with a descriptive phrase.

4. Point out that sometimes poets borrow patterns from other things like lists and puzzles for creating a poem. **Lead students in discussing the problem-solving process behind the puns and wordplay of this poem.** For example, *Footwhere* is a play on the word "footwear," referring to shoes, but adding "where" instead of "wear" to communicate the idea of "lost" in the phrase *lost shoe*. Deconstruct each of the words in column 2 together with students. Then read the whole poem aloud again.

5. Follow with more one-worders by **J. Patrick Lewis in "Food One-Worders"** (6th Grade, Week 11, page 49), or selections from *Lemonade: and Other Poems Squeezed from a Single Word* by Bob Raczka.

WEEK 26: NONSENSE

ONE-WORDERS
by **J. Patrick Lewis**

Lost shoe	→	Footwhere
#1 eye doctor	→	Toptometrist
What a guillotine does	→	Disconnecks
Porcupine's nickname	→	Lancelot
Cattle farm fence	→	Boundairy
Bungee jumper	→	Boyo-yo
Antarctic survivor	→	Pengwin
Joey's house	→	Kangaroom
Dog bath	→	Chihuahuash
Pet entrance	→	Labradoor
Doggie park	→	Terriertory
Chicken nuggets	→	Cock-a-doodle-doom
February 14th love song	→	Valentune
Speed read	→	Gobble-de-book
Arithmetic whiz	→	Mathlete
Two skydivers	→	Pairachutists
Ship sailing yeastward	→	Mayflour
One-fifth of a house	→	Two-tents
World's biggest telescope	→	Vastronomer
The Wordplay's the Thing	→	Shakespirit

WEEK 27: WORLD OF WORDS

EIGHTH GRADE

Take 5!

1. **If you have a paper of your own that you have written that includes scribbles, arrows, or editorial marks, show it as an example of a draft of writing.** Then read the poem aloud.

2. For a follow-up reading, **invite a team of volunteers to work with you to prepare a scripted reading.** Many of the lines of the poem are questions, so one or more volunteers could read those lines while the rest of the volunteers read the declarative statements with you. You can also vary readers by stanza, if you have enough volunteers. Then read the poem aloud at a fairly quick pace for greater impact.

3. **Talk about the standard proofreader's marks that real copyeditors use to correct a work of writing.** Which are familiar and which are new to students? Post them for future reference. One possible source is Merriam-Webster.com/mw/table/proofrea.htm.

4. Talk with students about how the reader or listener knows whose point of view is presented in the poem. (It's not the poet's point of view!) What is the poet trying to say here? (She is expressing frustration with the abundance of input from an editor, much of it random and contradictory.) **How does the poet use dramatic irony to make a point? (Consider the title, which refers to ten drafts over a four-year period, as well as the final stanza, which begins with a paradoxical line:** *I'm not even sure I like him. / This book will be great.***)** Then read the poem aloud again.

5. Share another poem about getting words right, **"Breaking the Spell" by Debbie Levy** (7th Grade, Week 27, page 157), or selections from *Time You Let Me In* or *Salting the Ocean*, edited by Naomi Shihab Nye.

EDITORIAL SUGGESTIONS
(On 10th Draft, After 4 Years)
by Naomi Shihab Nye

Your narrator needs to sound older.
What is he, 8? Could he be more sophisticated?
Does he have ADD? Do you know who he is?
This book feels lost. Adrift, on the waves.

It needs to be longer. Give us a handle.
The story feels distant somehow but we want
to feel close. We must walk on that beach with them
from the inside. Does this make sense?

Your time is all over the map. What day is it?
Is this happening in one day? One week?
Do you know where we are? Don't report on details.
Details drive the action. Each chapter must be
a self-contained unit. Lead us on.

But put a harness on every chapter. The fishing chapter,
they could really catch a fish. I mean, why not?
The boy—what is his name?—his personality needs to be clearer.
He can't be coy. We need to fall in love with him. Right now

I'm not even sure I like him. This book will be great.
We need it to be more exciting, not jumpy.
Focus. Maybe you could have a stone in every chapter.
Let the stone be the centerpiece. Would that work?

WEEK 28: BOOKS

EIGHTH GRADE

Take 5!

1. **Pile together a variety of books of all kinds and place them in front of you as a poetry prop.** Then read the poem aloud slowly.

2. **Invite three students to join you in reading the poem aloud again.** (They can each choose a partner if needed for extra confidence.) Each student or pair will read one of the words/phrases in line 3 (*agendas* or *philosophies* or *belief systems*) while you read the rest of the poem aloud. Be sure to coach them on saying the word slowly and emphatically, with each student or pair pausing between each word.

3. **Collaborate with students to make a list of some of their favorite authors and poets.** Post the list on the door to share with others.

4. Sometimes poets use exaggeration to add impact to their poems. **This use of figurative language is called hyperbole. Discuss this element with students and identify its use in this poem** (*for the rest of my life* and *so they don't get in my brain*). Why did the poet use hyperbole in this poem in this way? (Underlining the impossibility of the resolution to keep ideas out of your brain.) Then read the poem aloud again.

5. Connect this poem with another about a teacher, **"What She Asked" by Virginia Euwer Wolff** (7th Grade, Week 2, page 107), and share "Advanced English" and other selections from *Blue Lipstick: Concrete Poems* by John Grandits.

My English Teacher
by **Lorie Ann Grover**

She teaches me
authors have
agendas, philosophies, belief systems
leaking through their words
even if they don't know it

I will be watching
for the rest of my life
so they don't get in my brain
without me
ever knowing it

WEEK 29: POETRY POEMS — EIGHTH GRADE

Take 5!

1. If possible, **bring a branch or tree limb or a single rose as a poetry prop to set the stage for this poem.** Then read the poem aloud, emphasizing the words in italics.

2. **Recruit six volunteers to help you read the poem aloud a second time.** Each volunteer takes one of the words in italics while you read the rest of the poem aloud.

3. **Talk with students about "clichés" and how the poet pushes the reader to go beyond using ordinary words and expressions.** What examples of poetic clichés are noted in the poem? (Poems are NOT only about sunsets, birdsong, blossoms, cats, and roses, for example.)

4. In creating fresh images, poets often use sensory language to paint a picture in your mind. **Talk with students about how key words are used in this poem to evoke the senses,** and challenge them to identify particular examples from the poem (e.g., *blue, sunrise, sunset, day breaks, night collapses, cold air, song, noise, glitters,* and so on). After this discussion, share the whole poem aloud again.

5. Follow this poem with **"Meet The Saurus" by Heidi Mordhorst** (6th Grade, Week 28, page 83), or selections from *Borrowed Names: Poems about Laura Ingalls Wilder, Madam C.J. Walker, Marie Curie, and Their Daughters*, also by Jeannine Atkins.

A CONVERSATION BETWEEN POETS
by Jeannine Atkins

Say anything, but be leery of words
too common in the trade. *Bells, begone*,
even *blue* should be used with caution.
Avoid *sunrise, sunset,* and *apple blossoms.*
It's better to find new words
for where day breaks or night collapses.
Consider the fruit tree not in bloom, but after leaves
drop and gray boughs twist through cold air.

I'm sorry to tell you that the birds will have to go.
We hear their song, yes, but they've been
making noise too long. Skimp on what glitters.
Be prudent describing the acrobatics
of cats. If you insist on roses, hum
about thorns as well as petals.

Week 30: Rhyme, Repetition, & Rhythm

Eighth Grade

Take 5!

1. **Hold a journal or notebook labeled "PRIVATE" as your poetry prop** while you read this poem aloud.

2. **Invite students to select their favorite line and to chime in on that line only**, alone or with a partner, while you read the whole poem aloud.

3. For discussion: *What are the pros and cons of keeping a journal?*

4. Repetition is often a key ingredient in creating poems. **Sometimes a poet uses repetition not just to enhance the sound of the poem, but to emphasize meaning, too.** Lead the students in discussing how the poet repeats the same basic sentence structure for each line by beginning with *I'm* or *I* (suggesting diary-like entries and introspection). Consider the poet's use of rhyme (every two even-numbered lines rhyme) to tie this "list" poem together, too. Then read the poem aloud again.

5. Connect to another poem by **Betsy Franco, "Fourths of Me"** (7th Grade, Week 30, page 163), or selections from her novel in verse, *Metamorphosis: Junior Year*.

IN CASE YOU'RE READING MY JOURNAL . . . I'LL SUMMARIZE
by **Betsy Franco**

I'm dreaming about him.
I don't know where I'm at.
I'm wretched cuz of this.
I'm blissing out on that.
I'm miserable at times.
I'm always quite confused.
I'm mad you're in my face.
I'm really not amused.
I'm smarter than you think.
I'm sadder than I show.
I'm hoping against hope.
I'm guessing he must know.
I'm trying to be me.
I'm mystified by that.
I'm doing all I can.
I'm really not a brat.

WEEK 31: DIFFERENT FORMS

EIGHTH GRADE

Take 5!

1. **Display the word "transdifferentiation" before reading the poem aloud, pausing significantly between the two stanzas.** Then look up the meaning of this key, italicized word together. (The rare natural transformation of cells other than stem cells into a different type of cell; current uses show potential for gene therapy and new drug discoveries.)

2. For this unique poem, **invite students to choose their favorite line from the first stanza and then join in on that line** when it occurs in both the first stanza and the second stanza. You take the lead and read the entire poem while students join in on their selected line.

3. Do a bit of quick collaborative research on what we know about the jellyfish and discuss your findings briefly. Why did the poet entitle the poem "Immortal?" **Point out that sometimes poets weave facts into their poems, and guide students in noting what factual information we glean from this poem.**

4. Poets enjoy experimenting with writing poetry in different forms and formats. **One new approach developed by poet Marilyn Singer is the "reverso" poem, really two poems that employ the same words (with changes only in punctuation and capitalization), arranged in the opposite order for completely different meanings.** Guide the students in understanding this form using the two examples here, line by line. Then read the poem aloud again together.

5. Revisit another poem about a small sea creature, **"Leafy Sea Dragon" by Steven Withrow** (8th Grade, Week 7, page 193), or follow this poem with more examples of the reverso form created by Marilyn Singer in *Mirror Mirror: A Book of Reversible Verse* and *Follow Follow: A Book of Reverso Poems*.

IMMORTAL
by Kristy Dempsey

Back and forth
this jellyfish grows ...
maturing
reverting,
(growing,
ungrowing)
specialized cells
escaping danger
by *transdifferentiation*.
A polyp,
morphs to hydroid, then becomes
Medusa with bell and tentacles.
Sensing danger, it transforms backwards.
This jellyfish might know
how to live forever.

How to live forever?
This jellyfish might know:
sensing danger, it transforms backwards.
Medusa with bell and tentacles
morphs to hydroid then becomes
a polyp
by *transdifferentiation*.
Escaping danger,
specialized cells
ungrowing,
growing
reverting,
maturing ...
this jellyfish grows
back and forth.

WEEK 32: METAPHOR & SIMILE — EIGHTH GRADE

Take 5!

1. **Bring bread-related props (*bread, toast, butter, honey, jam*) and place them prominently while you read the poem aloud**, pausing briefly between each stanza.

2. Next, **recruit four or more volunteers to join you in reading the poem aloud**. Each volunteer or small group can take one stanza and read it aloud with you, with or without the bread-themed props.

3. **Poll students on their favorite kinds of bread**: loaves, toast, rolls, baguettes, tortillas, Chinese buns, and so on.

4. In building a poem, poets often use metaphors to compare one thing to another to give us a fresh perspective on both things. **Lead students in identifying the extended metaphor woven throughout this poem.** What two things are being compared to one another (bread and people)? Discuss the attributes they share and the clever way the poet uses bread-related words (***crusty** old heel, **half-baked** ideas, **loaf** around*, etc.). Then read the whole poem aloud again.

5. Follow with another poem by **Lesléa Newman, "Mangoes"** (7th Grade, Week 31, page 165), or revisit another metaphorical poem, **"Safe in My Shell" by Ann Whitford Paul** (8th Grade, Week 6, page 191).

According to Bread
by Lesléa Newman

I may be a crusty old heel
full of half-baked ideas
I may loaf around
and do a crummy job

We both know
I always need dough
and more often than not
my life is toast

So tear me apart
eat me alive
swallow me whole
or punch me down

as long as you butter me up
and knead me, honey
whenever you're in a jam
I will rise

Week 33: Personification

Eighth Grade

Take 5!

1. Before reading this poem, alert students to the "gross" factor in this poem, which should tantalize them further! Then **read the poem aloud, using extra emphasis for the words referring to body parts**.

2. This time, **invite students to choose their favorite body part mentioned in the poem** (*heart, liver, kidney, lungs, intestines, entrails, guts, spleen, intestine, pancreas*) and join in on saying that word while you read the rest of the poem aloud.

3. **Students will surely want to discuss the term "eviscerate,"** often associated with warfare and, now, video games.

4. Poets often use elements of figurative language like personification to create a vivid poem. **Lead students in discussing how this poet has given the verb "eviscerate" a female persona along with human qualities**, and challenge them to identify those qualities specifically with words and phrases from the poem (*the gal for you; She'll reach inside; She'll wave; she'll wear as a scarf,* etc.). Finally, read the poem aloud again.

5. Read another poem by **Michael Salinger, "Gear"** (7th Grade, Week 24, page 151), or follow with more poems about the human body in *The Blood-Hungry Spleen and Other Poems about Our Parts* by Allan Wolf.

EVISCERATE
by Michael Salinger

Eviscerate likes to get to the heart of a matter
Along with the liver, kidney, lungs and intestines too
If it entails entrails
Eviscerate is the gal for you
She'll reach inside and pull out your guts
Making internal, external
She'll wave your spleen over her head
Skip rope with your large intestine
Your pancreas she'll wear as a scarf
One might question her intentions
But Eviscerate believes beyond any doubt
What was in should now be out.

Note: From the Latin *evisceratus*—the *e* meaning "ex or out" and *viscera* meaning "internal organs." So this word means out with internal organs.

WEEK 34: ON THE MOVE

EIGHTH GRADE

Take 5!

1. **To set the stage before reading this poem, go to Calm.com and project the scene there for a moment.** Then read the poem aloud with the image projected, but the sound muted.

2. **Invite two students to join you in sharing this poem aloud.** Collaborate with them on how to read the poem aloud again; perhaps each volunteer can read one of the first two pivotal lines, for example.

3. Talk with students about places they would like to go and **make a collaborative list of dream destinations.** For help, consult the book *1000 Places to See Before You Die*.

4. **This is a lyrical poem written in first person that considers how we may sometimes feel "restless" and want to be several places at once.** What thoughts or emotions does the poem prompt in us? Guide students in discussing which lines suggest how the poet feels in this poem. Consider the impact of the line breaks on the poem and contrast this with a look at the poem as if it were written in continuous prose (*I am not here. I am elsewhere. By those distant firs, perhaps. Stepping on a train, somewhere. Saying goodbye. Heading for the outskirts of the world. My voice, a plaintive cry. My body, an arrow of geese fleeing the autumn sky.*). Although her poem is only 42 words long, Sidman has created a poignant piece by her choice of voice, language, and format. Finally, read the poem aloud again.

5. Share another poem by **Joyce Sidman, "Convection"** (6th Grade, Week 30, page 87), or selections from *This Place I Know: Poems of Comfort,* edited by Georgia Heard.

THE POETRY FRIDAY ANTHOLOGY

RESTLESS
by Joyce Sidman

I am not here.
I am elsewhere.
By those distant firs, perhaps.
Stepping on a train, somewhere.
Saying goodbye.
Heading for the outskirts
of the world.
My voice, a plaintive cry.
My body,
an arrow of geese
fleeing the autumn sky.

Week 35: Summer Vacation

Eighth Grade

Take 5!

1. **Give yourself a mock bug bite tattoo with a red marker.** Rub it as if it were itchy as you prepare to read this poem aloud.

2. Prior to your follow-up reading, gather large chart paper or poster board and markers and **invite an artistic student to sketch a quick, Pictionary-style image suggested by the poem.** Read the poem aloud again while your volunteer draws the poem-picture in front of the students. Display a copy of the poem alongside the sketch.

3. Lead a discussion about the experience of reading or listening to this poem when you read it aloud in contrast with viewing a digital video of a "poem movie" adaptation. **Look for the video featuring this poem on the PFAMS blog (PFAMS.blogspot.com).** What is distinctive about each experience? What is similar? Then read the poem aloud together again.

4. **Poems usually rhyme at the end of lines, but sometimes they rhyme in the middle too, which is called internal rhyme.** Challenge the students to find the ending "slant" or "almost" rhyme (*muse/tattoos*), as well as the internal rhyming words in the lines of this poem (*suntan/and/sand; speckles/freckles*). For a bonus, see if they notice the use of alliteration, too, with the repetition of consonant sounds in stressed syllables (*s* in *season, stamps, summer; suntan, sand; streaks of sweat; seaweedy speckles, scores; t* in *temporary tattoos*). Then read the poem aloud one more time.

5. Revisit **"Sunbeam Confesses Its Love of Geometry" by Mary Lee Hahn** (8th Grade, Week 9, page 197), or selections from *How to Cross a Pond: Poems about Water* by Marilyn Singer or *Vacation: We're Going to the Ocean* by David L. Harrison.

Body Art
by Marilyn Singer

No season stamps me like summer—

    with suntan and sand,

        mosquito bites and streaks of sweat,

        seaweedy speckles, scores of freckles.

As August ends, I muse

    on just how much I'll miss

        these annoying or appealing

        temporary tattoos.

WEEK 36: LOOKING FORWARD

EIGHTH GRADE

Take 5!

1. Students may not be familiar with cod or fishing for cod, so **show an image before reading the poem aloud to help them visualize the poem's subject**. Possible sources to search include Photography.NationalGeographic.com or WorldFishingNetwork.com.

2. **Collaborate with students to create a slide show version of this poem.** Research five photos, one for each stanza in the poem—a deep sea fishing boat, a large cod (fish) caught on a fishing line, a girl being photographed with a prize fish, a bucket of rotting fish—ending with one image suggested by the powerful end line, *one day I will be captain of something,* and use that line as the caption for the image. Then read the poem aloud and record it to use as the narration for the slide show.

3. **Challenge students to consider what they might one day want to be "captain" of (figuratively speaking) and encourage them to put that dream in writing.** Gather and store them in a "time capsule" for the future.

4. **This poem is an example of a narrative poem—a poem that tells a story complete with characters, conflict, setting, and theme.** Help students identify each of those components in this particular poem. Guide students in seeing how the lines and line breaks build the poem, particularly how the poet uses shorter lines to heighten the action on the boat and in catching the big fish. Consider the poet's choices in minimal punctuation and capitalization, too—the concept of "poetic license" to manipulate the conventions of written speech. Then read the poem aloud again or view the student-created slide show version.

5. Connect this poem with another fishing poem, **"Fishing Trip" by Charles Waters** (6th Grade, Week 17, page 61), or selections from *Amaze Me* by Naomi Shihab Nye.

Cod
by Holly Thompson

she was pleased to get
the morning off babysitting
and signed up for deep sea fishing
proud to be the only girl on board
glad to prove she could pierce worms
with hooks and wield the rods
and keep her footing and not go green
on the rise and fall of swells

that was enough
so what happened was a bonus
the weight on the line
the captain's confirmation
the slow reeling in
the magnificence of the spectacle
of the 36-inch cod flapping on deck

and when they docked
cameras clicking at her
holding up the boat hook
showing off the heavy fish
the captain promising
to fillet it, pack it and freeze it
so she could send it home
and eat baked cod all year
she could taste it already—
with a squeeze of lemon
on the buttery toasted breading

but late afternoon on her walk with the babies
when she strolled past a bar where the captain
sat laughing and from the pier looked down
to the floating dock and the tub full of fish
her cod on top sun bathed and rotting
its dim, milky eye focused on her, she realized

to be passenger or crew was not enough
and she promised the great Atlantic cod:
one day I will be captain of something

A Poem for Everyone

Take 5!

1. On a large piece of paper or on the chalkboard or whiteboard, make a "To Do" list. **Label it "To Do" or "Things to Do" and number it 1, 2, 3, and so on, leaving every line blank.** Then read the poem aloud slowly, particularly the last four lines.

2. For a follow-up reading, point out that lines 2, 3, 4, 5, 6, 7, and 8 list fun things to do once school is out (*I will sleep late; walk my dog; ride my bike; read for fun; play some tunes; text my friends; meet at the mall*). **Invite students to choose their favorite of those activities and chime in** on the one line that mentions that activity as you read the rest of the poem aloud.

3. **Work together to make a fun list of MORE things to do when school is out.** Challenge students to include "read poetry" or "write poetry" on their lists!

4. Poets choose and arrange each word carefully as they craft their poems. Guide the students in discussing how the poet turns this simple list into a poem by using effective line breaks to give the poem its rhythm. **Compare this with how the poem would look and sound if it were written as continuous prose**: *Tomorrow I will sleep late, walk my dog, ride my bike, read for fun, play some tunes, text my friends, meet at the mall . . . hey, wait, maybe I'll do nothing at all just because I can.* In only 36 words, the poet has created a poem by making clever use of line arrangement and spacing. Read the poem aloud again to get the full effect.

5. Revisit **Julie Larios's** poem, **"First Day at a New School,"** the very first poem in this book ("A Poem for Everyone," page 23). Talk about which Poetry Friday poems have been students' favorites this year.

THE LAST DAY OF SCHOOL
by **Stephanie Calmenson**

Tomorrow
I will sleep late,
walk my dog,
ride my bike,
read for fun,
play some tunes,
text my friends,
meet at the mall . . .
hey, wait,
maybe I'll do
nothing at all
just
because
I
can.

*"For what is a poem but a hazardous attempt at self-understanding: it is **the deepest part of autobiography.**"*

❧ Robert Penn Warren ☙

More Poetry Resources

Building Your Own Poetry Library

How do we identify which poetry books are the best for young people or most useful in the 6-8 classroom? One of the best places to begin is by looking at poetry award winners.

The **Children's Poet Laureate** (CPL) was established by the Poetry Foundation in 2006 to raise awareness of the fact that young people have a natural receptivity to poetry and are its most appreciative audience, especially when poems are written specifically for them. The Children's Poet Laureate serves as a consultant to the Foundation and gives public readings. The first CPL was Jack Prelutsky, followed by Mary Ann Hoberman and J. Patrick Lewis.

Another major award for poetry for children is **the National Council of Teachers of English (NCTE) Award for Excellence in Poetry for Children**, given to a poet for her or his entire body of work in writing or anthologizing poetry for children. Several of the winners are included in this anthology: X.J. Kennedy, Nikki Grimes, J. Patrick Lewis, and Joyce Sidman. Any book of poetry by one of these award winners will be worthwhile.

> **Your Poetry Checklist**
>
> ☑ Highlight poetry books on the chalk rail, shelf top, table, or website
>
> ☑ Seek out poetry books from diverse perspectives
>
> ☑ Link poems with novels and nonfiction
>
> ☑ Connect children's poetry with history, science, and mathematics
>
> ☑ Tell your colleagues about Poetry Friday!

Other prominent awards include The **Lee Bennett Hopkins Award** for Children's Poetry, which is presented annually to an American poet or anthologist for the most outstanding new book of poetry for young people published in the previous year; the **Claudia Lewis Award,** given by Bank Street College for the best poetry book of the year; and **The Lion and the Unicorn Award** for Excellence in North American Poetry for the best poetry book published in either the U.S. or Canada. A detailed listing of major poetry awards, past winners, and useful award-related website links can be found in *The Poetry Teacher's Book of Lists* by Sylvia Vardell.

The Poetry Teacher's Book of Lists also offers input on selecting poetry for young people ages 0-18. It contains 155 different lists and cites nearly 1500 poetry books in a variety of categories including:

- Poetry Awards and "Best" Lists
- Seasonal and Holiday Poetry Booklists (such as Valentine's, Earth Day, Halloween, etc.)

- Multicultural and International Poetry Booklists (such as African American or bilingual poetry books)

- Thematic or Topical Poetry Booklists (humor, family, friendship, coping, etc.)

- Poetry Booklists Across the Curriculum (animals, food, math, science, history, etc.)

- Poetry Booklists Highlighting the Form of Poetry (limericks, acrostics, haiku, etc.)

- Strategies for Creating a Poetry-Friendly Environment (poetry displays and quotes, lesson plan tips, a poetry scavenger hunt, poet birthdays)

- Strategies for Sharing and Responding to Poetry Out Loud (poetry performance tips, assessment rubrics, discussion prompts)

- Strategies for Teaching Poetry Writing (books with poet commentary, poetry written by young people, lists of poem forms, writers' checklists)

- General Poetry Teaching Resources (poetry websites and blogs, poetry text sets, reference tools)

If you are looking for poetry books for Mother's Day or graduation, or poems about war or presidents, for example, you'll find lists for each of those and more.

Poetry Websites and Blogs

As we look for new places for poetry to pop up, you can be sure that this includes the Internet. There are several hundred websites and blogs that make poems available; these often include audio and video recordings of poets reading their poems and/or biographical information about poets, too. A comprehensive list of poetry websites and blogs can be found in *The Poetry Teacher's Book of Lists* as well as on Sylvia Vardell's Poetry For Children blog.

Most of the established poetry blogs participate in the "Poetry Friday" celebration, posting a poem or poetry-related items on Fridays. Some include teaching activities and even welcome student participation. Sites and blogs also offer links to additional poetry resources on the web. Here is a select list of electronic resources that are particularly helpful in sharing poetry with young people.

25 Poetry Websites and Blogs You Need to Know

About Poetry:

Alphabet Soup
by Jama Rattigan
JamaRattigan.com

The Academy of American Poets
Poets.org

Columbia Granger's World of Poetry
ColumbiaGrangers.org

Favorite Poem Project
FavoritePoem.org

The Miss Rumphius Effect
by Tricia Stohr-Hunt
MissRumphiusEffect.Blogspot.com

The Library of Congress Poetry and Literature Center
LOC.gov/poetry

No Water River
NoWaterRiver.com

Poetry Alive
PoetryAlive.com

Poetry for Children
by Sylvia Vardell
PoetryForChildren.Blogspot.com

Poetry Daily
Poems.com

Poetry Foundation
PoetryFoundation.org

Poetry At Play: Poetry Advocates for Children and Young Adults
PoetryatPlay.org

Poetry Out Loud
PoetryOutLoud.org

Poetry Slams, Inc.
PoetrySlam.com

Poetry Speaks
PoetrySpeaks.com

Teen Ink Magazine
TeenInk.com

A Year of Reading
by Franki Sibberson
& Mary Lee Hahn
ReadingYear.Blogspot.com

Poets:

April Halprin Wayland
AprilHalprinWayland.com

David L. Harrison's blog
DavidLHarrison.Wordpress.com

The Drift Record
by Julie Larios
JulieLarios.Blogspot.com

GottaBook
by Greg Pincus
Gottabook.Blogspot.com

Nikki Sounds Off
by Nikki Grimes
NikkiGrimes.com/blog

The Poem Farm
by Amy Ludwig VanDerwater
PoemFarm.AmyLV.com

Poetry Suitcase
by Janet Wong
PoetrySuitcase.com

Writing the World for Kids
by Laura Purdie Salas
LauraSalas.Wordpress.com

E-Resources for Poetry Teaching

One of the most controversial topics in the world of reading today concerns e-books. Some people think that e-books will replace paper books and change the way we read—and they're afraid of those changes. We agree that changes will happen, but we're excited by the possibilities. Consider:

- a teacher can read a book review at lunch and buy an e-book version of it (for less than the price of lunch);

- that book might be a collection of poems from Mexico or Australia but is delivered immediately without shipping costs or custom fees;

- the teacher can download the e-book onto an e-reader and also a regular computer that can be projected onto a screen for the whole class to read aloud together;

- e-resources are easily searchable. A teacher can look for a poem using keywords like *family* or *armadillo*. Even if you prefer paper books, you might consider owning a second copy that is digital as a teaching resource;

- and reluctant readers (who might not like paper books but might enjoy manipulating text on a screen) can read the book using electronic bookmarks, a glossary, and sometimes read-aloud features, too.

If you want to try an e-book and need to know where to get started, you'll find some titles and resources here:

PoetryforChildren.Blogspot.com

The Poetry Friday Anthology Blogs:
PFAMS.blogspot.com (for grades 6-8)
PoetryFridayAnthology.Blogspot.com (for K-5)

The PoetryTagTime Blogs:
PoetryGiftTag.Blogspot.com
PoetryTagTime.Blogspot.com
TeenPoetryTagTime.Blogspot.com

PoetryTeachersBookofLists.Blogspot.com

Professional Resource Books

This abbreviated list of professional reference sources will provide additional background that you will find helpful in selecting and sharing poetry with young people. For further reading, you will find several dozen professional resources listed in The Poetry Teacher's Book of Lists.

Ambrosini, Michelle and Morretta, Teresa. *Poetry Workshop for Middle School.*

Chatton, Barbara. *Using Poetry Across the Curriculum.*

Collom, Jack and Noethe, Sheryl. *Poetry Everywhere: Teaching Poetry Writing in School and in the Community.*

Franco, Betsy. *Conversations With a Poet: Inviting Poetry into K-12 Classrooms.*

Hanauer, David Ian. *Poetry and the Meaning of Life: Reading and Writing Poetry in Language Arts Classrooms.*

Heard, Georgia. *Awakening the Heart: Exploring Poetry in Elementary and Middle School.*

Holbrook, Sara. *Practical Poetry: A Nonstandard Approach to Meeting Content-Area Standards.*

Holbrook, Sara and Salinger, Michael. *Outspoken: How to Improve Writing and Speaking Through Poetry Performance.*

Hopkins, Lee. Bennett. *Pass the Poetry Please.*

Janeczko, Paul B. *Reading Poetry in the Middle Grades: 20 Poems and Activities that Meet the Common Core Standards and Cultivate a Passion for Poetry.*

Kennedy, X. J. and Kennedy, Dorothy. *Knock at a Star.*

Livingston, Myra Cohn. *Poem-Making.*

Mahoney, Mary Pat. *Practical Poetry: A Guide for Teaching the Common Core Text Exemplars for Poetry in Grades 6-8.*

Partington, Richie. *I Second that Emotion: Sharing Children's and Young Adult Poetry: A 21st Century Guide for Teachers and Librarians.*

Stanley, Nile. *Creating Readers with Poetry.*

Tiedt, Iris McClellan. *Tiger Lilies, Toadstools, And Thunderbolts: Engaging K-8 Students With Poetry.*

Vardell, Sylvia M. *Poetry Aloud Here: Sharing Poetry with Children.*

Vardell, Sylvia M. *Poetry People: A Practical Guide to Children's Poets.*

Vardell, Sylvia M. *The Poetry Teacher's Book of Lists.*

Wood, Jaime R. *Living Voices: Multicultural Poetry in the Middle School Classroom.*

A Mini Glossary of Poetry Terms

It can be helpful to have a vocabulary for discussing poetry, but please don't let this aspect get in the way of enjoying poems. This is a short list of key terms used throughout the Take 5 activities.

Alliteration: The repetition of consonants for effect, particularly as the initial sound in a string of words

Couplet: Paired lines of verses, often rhyming

Free verse: Poetry that does not follow a set pattern or form and is usually irregular in line length

Haiku: A three-line poem of Japanese origin and usually about nature. The first and third lines generally have five syllables and the second line has seven.

Image: Words invoking or describing sensory perceptions; imagery is the collective term for images

Internal rhyme: The rhyming words within a line of poetry

Lyrical poem: Literally meaning "to be sung accompanied by the lyre"; lyric has come to mean a poem expressing the poet's emotions; some poets use the term "in the lyrical voice" to describe first-person poems full of reflection

Metaphor: A figure of speech in which one thing or idea is represented by implicit comparison with another

Meter: The pattern of stressed and unstressed syllables in verse creating a distinctive rhythm

Narrative poem: A poem that tells a story (often in third person)

Onomatopoeia: Words that capture the sounds they describe

Personification: Describing non-human things in human terms

Quatrain: A four-line stanza

Repetition: Sounds, words, phrases, or structures used again and again in a poem, usually for musical effect or enhanced meaning

Rhyme: The matching of sounds of syllables at the ends of lines of verse

Rhythm: The pattern of beats or stresses in a line of poetry, conveying a sense of movement or sound

Simile: An explicit comparison between two things or ideas, usually using "as" or "like"

Sonnet: Typically a poem of fourteen lines using any of a number of formal rhyme schemes and often having ten syllables per line.

Stanza: A group of poetic lines often repeated according to a fixed pattern throughout a poem

Tercet: A three-line stanza

About the Poets

Biographical information, photos, and lists of some of the published titles of each of our contributing poets can be found at our website, www.PomeloBooks.com. Students might find it interesting, for instance, that Jack Prelutsky collects frog miniatures and April Halprin Wayland was once an aqua farmer!

Most poets have their own websites, too, where you can find contact info for them as well as news about their books and even links to their blogs. Some particularly useful poets' blogs can be found in our list of *25 Poetry Websites and Blogs You Need to Know* on page 258.

If you identified "favorite poets" when reading the poems in this anthology, you might want to contact them about speaking at your school—either in person or via video chat—or participating in a conference for teachers. Some poets enjoy large assemblies, some prefer small workshops, and some do both. Contact them and start a conversation!

Index and Credits

Copyright and Permissions

For permission to reprint any of the poems in this book, please contact the individual poets listed here either directly or through their agents.

Most of these poets can be reached through their individual websites, which are listed at our Pomelo Books website, www.PomeloBooks.com. If you need help getting in touch with a poet, just let us know and we'll be happy to connect you.

A note on copyright:

If it doesn't feel right to copy it . . . please *don't!*

Poets (like plumbers and lawyers and teachers and acrobats) need to earn a living from their work; permissions fees and royalties help pay the rent!

Title Index

A
According to Bread 243
Ack! 81
Advice to Rapunzel 69
After the Blizzard, Outside My Window 121
Another New Year 105
Ars Poetica 167

B
Biking Along White Rim Road 109
Bilingual 173
Black Ice 171
Body Art 249
Boy, The 223
Braces 201
Breaking the Spell 157

C
Café, The 205
Cat Hockey 35
Cod 251
Community Service 207
Company 147
Consider the Bombardier Beetle 39
Convection 87
Conversation Between Poets, A 237
Council of Brothers 225
Cousins 97

D
Deaf Boy, The 153
Dear Monster of Loch Ness 41
Doors of the 24-Hour Emergency Veterinary Hospital 189
Dracula 137
Dromedary Ferry 73

E
Editorial Suggestions 233
Eviscerate 245

F
Fear Factor, The 169
Feather 115
First Day at a New School 23
First Practice 55
First Week of School 29
Fishing Trip 61
5 O'clock Shadow 215
Fixer-Upper 127
Food Fest 199
Food One-Worders 49
For Bucky 187
Fourths of Me 163
Future Hoopsters 89

G
Gear 151
Giving 57
Goldfish 111
Grandma's House 129

H
He Was So Little 37
Her Room 203
How Romantic Can You Get? 221
How Tall Is the Boy? 139

I
I Had a Nightmare 217
I Know I'm Going Somewhere 99
Immortal 241
In Case You're Reading My Journal . . . I'll Summarize 239
In the Bog 155
In the School Band 183
In the Word Woods 85

J
Just Wanted to Tell You 143

L
Last Day of School, The 253
Leafy Sea Dragon 193
Light Reaction, A 65
Lost 71
Locker Ness Monster 31
Look My Way 145

M
Mangoes 165
Meet The Saurus 83
Mere Shadow 79
Miss Zayd's Oxford Shoes 211
Mom Talk 53
Monday's Cat 113
Movies of Us 213
My English Teacher 235

N
Names 47
Night Light 43

O
One-Worders 231
Opening Night 77

P
Pen 93
Perfect Day, A 219

R
Racing the Clouds 45
Restless 247
Rhapsody 229
Run, The 185

S
Safe in My Shell 191
Saved by the Book 161
Saying No 125
Screen Resolution 227
Season to Forgive 135

Shark, The 117
Shell, The 209
Silence 75
Sitting for Trishie Devlin 131
Sixth Grade Art Class 67
Spiral Glide 119
Sunbeam Confesses Its Love
   of Geometry 197

T
Texas, Out Driving 95
That Boat 91
These Hands 133
Tryouts 33
Turkey Vulture 195

W
Waking House, The 51
Way You Might Judge, The 181
What I Want to Be 123
What She Asked 107
Who Am I? 141
Wilbur Asks Charlotte Ten
   Questions 159
Wong's Café 59
World According to Climbers,
   The 149
World Cup 175

Y
Your Appendix Is a Mystery 63

Poet Index

A
Acey, Joy 139
Atkins, Jeannine 237

B
Bernier-Grand, Carmen T. 137
Black, Robyn Hood 31, 145
Brown, Calef 155
Bruchac, Joseph 171
Bryant, Jen 33, 175
Bulion, Leslie 195

C
Calmenson, Stephanie 253
Chandra, Deborah 209
Coombs, Kate 71, 129
Cotten, Cynthia 81

D
Dempsey, Kristy 53, 241

E
Engle, Margarita 141, 173

F
Franco, Betsy 163, 239

G
Gerber, Carole 43
Ghigna, Charles 51
Graham, Joan Bransfield 111
Grimes, Nikki 93
Grover, Lorie Ann 235
Gunning, Monica 211

H
Hahn, Mary Lee 119, 197
Harley, Avis 89, 185
Harrison, David L. 37, 183
Harshman, Terry Webb 127
Havill, Juanita 73
Heard, Georgia 167
Hemphill, Stephanie 229
Holbrook, Sara 169
Hoyte, Carol-Ann 65
Hubbell, Patricia 143

J
Jules, Jacqueline 45, 227

K
Kennedy, X.J. 117
Kulp, Linda 75

L
Larios, Julie 23, 47, 219
Latham, Irene 109, 149
LaTulippe, Renée M. 77, 133
Levine, Gail Carson 147
Levy, Debbie 157
Lewis, J. Patrick 49, 231
Lyon, George Ella 91, 161, 221

M
McCall, Guadalupe Garcia 205, 223
Mordhorst, Heidi 83

N
Nelson, Marilyn 153, 225
Newman, Lesléa 121, 165, 243
Nye, Naomi Shihab 95, 187, 233

P
Paul, Ann Whitford 191
Prelutsky, Jack 41

Q
Quattlebaum, Mary 123, 201

R
Roemer, Heidi Bee 199
Rosen, Michael J. 113, 213
Ruddell, Deborah 67

S
Salas, Laura Purdie 203
Salinger, Michael 151, 245
Scheu, Ted 99
Sidman, Joyce 87, 247
Singer, Marilyn 115, 249
Slesarik, Ken 135
Sones, Sonya 131
Spinelli, Eileen 69

T
Thompson, Holly 251

V
VanDerwater, Amy Ludwig 55, 125

W
Wardlaw, Lee 35
Waters, Charles 61, 97, 215
Wayland, April Halprin 85, 217
Weinstock, Robert 79
Withrow, Steven 193
Wolf, Allan 63
Wolff, Virginia Euwer 107, 189
Wong, Janet 29, 59, 105, 181, 207

Y
Yolen, Jane 39, 57, 159

Poem Credits

Joy Acey: "How Tall Is the Boy?" (7th Grade, Week 18: Human Body); copyright ©2013 by Joy Acey. Used with permission of the author. All rights reserved.

Jeannine Atkins: "A Conversation Between Poets" (8th Grade, Week 29: Poetry Poems); copyright ©2013 by Jeannine Atkins. Used with permission of the author. All rights reserved.

Carmen T. Bernier-Grand: "Dracula" (7th Grade, Week 17: Time Together); copyright ©2013 by Carmen T. Bernier-Grand. Used with permission of the author. All rights reserved.

Robyn Hood Black: "Locker Ness Monster" (6th Grade, Week 2: More School), "Look My Way" (7th Grade, Week 21: Love & Friendship); copyright ©2013 by Robyn Hood Black. Used with permission of the author. All rights reserved.

Calef Brown: "In the Bog" (7th Grade, Week 26: Nonsense); copyright ©2013 by Calef Brown. Used with permission of the author. All rights reserved.

Joseph Bruchac: "Black Ice" (7th Grade, Week 34: On the Move); copyright ©2013 by Joseph Bruchac. Used with permission of the author. All rights reserved.

Jen Bryant: "Tryouts" (6th Grade, Week 3: Fun & Games), "World Cup" (7th Grade, Week 36: Looking Forward); copyright ©2013 by Jen Bryant. Used with permission of the author. All rights reserved.

Leslie Bulion: "Turkey Vulture" (8th Grade, Week 8: In the Air); copyright ©2013 by Leslie Bulion. Used with permission of the author. All rights reserved.

Stephanie Calmenson: "The Last Day of School" (A Poem for Everyone); copyright ©2013 by Stephanie Calmenson. Used with permission of the author. All rights reserved.

Deborah Chandra: "The Shell" (8th Grade, Week 15: Stuff We Love); copyright ©2013 by Deborah Chandra. Used with permission of the author. All rights reserved.

Kate Coombs: "Lost" (6th Grade, Week 22: A Kinder Place), "Grandma's House" (7th Grade, Week 13: Families); copyright ©2013 by Kate Coombs. Used with permission of the author. All rights reserved.

Cynthia Cotten: "Ack!" (6th Grade, Week 27: World of Words); copyright ©2013 by Cynthia Cotten. Used with permission of the author. All rights reserved.

Kristy Dempsey: "Mom Talk" (6th Grade, Week 13: Families), "Immortal" (8th Grade, Week 31: Different Forms); copyright ©2013 by Kristy Dempsey. Used with permission of the author. All rights reserved.

Margarita Engle: "Who Am I?" (7th Grade, Week 19: More Human Body), "Bilingual" (7th Grade, Week 35: Summer Vacation); copyright ©2013 by Margarita Engle. Used with permission of the author. All rights reserved.

Betsy Franco: "Fourths of Me" (7th Grade, Week 30: Rhyme, Repetition, & Rhythm), "In Case You're Reading My Journal . . . I'll Summarize" (8th Grade, Week 30: Rhyme, Repetition, & Rhythm); copyright ©2013 by Betsy Franco. Used with permission of the author. All rights reserved.

Carole Gerber: "Night Light" (6th Grade, Week 8: In the Air); copyright ©2013 by Carole Gerber. Used with permission of the author. All rights reserved.

Charles Ghigna: "The Waking House" (6th Grade, Week 12: House & Home); copyright ©2013 by Charles Ghigna. Used with permission of the author. All rights reserved.

Joan Bransfield Graham: "Goldfish" (7th Grade, Week 4: Pets); copyright ©2013 by Joan Bransfield Graham. Used with permission of the author. All rights reserved.

Nikki Grimes: "Pen" (6th Grade, Week 33: Personification); copyright ©2013 by Nikki Grimes. Used with permission of Curtis Brown, Ltd. All rights reserved.

Lorie Ann Grover: "My English Teacher" (8th Grade, Week 28: Books); copyright ©2013 by Lorie Ann Grover. Used with permission of Curtis Brown, Ltd. All rights reserved.

Monica Gunning: "Miss Zayd's Oxford Shoes" (8th Grade, Week 16: Holidays); copyright ©2013 by Monica Gunning. Used with permission of the author. All rights reserved.

Mary Lee Hahn: "Spiral Glide" (7th Grade, Week 8: In the Air), "Sunbeam Confesses Its Love of Geometry" (8th Grade, Week 9: Weather); copyright ©2013 by Mary Lee Hahn. Used with permission of the author. All rights reserved.

Avis Harley: "Future Hoopsters" (6th Grade, Week 31: Different Forms), "The Run" (8th Grade, Week 3: Fun & Games); copyright ©2013 by Avis Harley. Used with permission of the author. All rights reserved.

David L. Harrison: "He Was So Little" (6th Grade, Week 5: More Pets), "In the School Band" (8th Grade, Week 2: More School); copyright ©2013 by David L. Harrison. Used with permission of the author. All rights reserved.

Terry Webb Harshman: "Fixer-Upper" (7th Grade, Week 12: House & Home); copyright ©2013 by Terry Webb Harshman. Used with permission of the author. All rights reserved.

Juanita Havill: "Dromedary Ferry" (6th Grade, Week 23: Exploring); copyright ©2013 by Juanita Havill. Used with permission of the author. All rights reserved.

Georgia Heard: "Ars Poetica" (7th Grade, Week 32: Metaphor & Simile); copyright ©2013 by Georgia Heard. Used with permission of the author. All rights reserved.

Stephanie Hemphill: "Rhapsody" (8th Grade, Week 25: Song & Dance); copyright ©2013 by Stephanie Hemphill. Used with permission of the author. All rights reserved.

Sara Holbrook: "The Fear Factor" (7th Grade, Week 33: Personification); copyright ©2013 by Sara Holbrook. Used with permission of the author. All rights reserved.

Carol-Ann Hoyte: "A Light Reaction" (6th Grade, Week 19: More Human Body); copyright ©2013 by Carol-Ann Hoyte. Used with permission of the author. All rights reserved.

Patricia Hubbell: "Just Wanted to Tell You" (7th Grade, Week 20: Art & Colors); copyright ©2013 by Patricia Hubbell. Used with permission of the author. All rights reserved.

Jacqueline Jules: "Racing the Clouds" (6th Grade, Week 9: Weather), "Screen Resolution" (8th Grade, Week 24: Science & Technology); copyright ©2013 by Jacqueline Jules. Used with permission of the author. All rights reserved.

X.J. Kennedy "The Shark" (7th Grade, Week 7: In the Water); copyright ©2013 by X.J. Kennedy. Used with permission of Curtis Brown, Ltd. All rights reserved.

Linda Kulp: "Silence" (6th Grade, Week 24: Science & Technology); copyright ©2013 by Linda Kulp. Used with permission of the author. All rights reserved.

Julie Larios: "First Day at a New School" (A Poem for Everyone), "Names" (6th Grade, Week 10: Food), "A Perfect Day" (8th Grade, Week 20: Art & Colors); copyright ©2013 by Julie Larios. Used with permission of the author. All rights reserved.

Irene Latham: "Biking Along White Rim Road" (7th Grade, Week 3: Fun & Games), "The World According to Climbers" (7th Grade, Week 23: Exploring); copyright ©2013 by Irene Latham. Used with permission of the author. All rights reserved.

Renée M. LaTulippe: "Opening Night" (6th Grade, Week 25: Song & Dance), "These Hands" (7th Grade, Week 15: Stuff We Love); copyright ©2013 by Renée M. LaTulippe. Used with permission of the author. All rights reserved.

Gail Carson Levine: "Company" (7th Grade, Week 22: A Kinder Place); copyright ©2013 by Gail Carson Levine. Used with permission of Curtis Brown, Ltd. All rights reserved.

Debbie Levy: "Breaking the Spell" (7th Grade, Week 27: World of Words); copyright ©2013 by Debbie Levy. Used with permission of the author. All rights reserved.

J. Patrick Lewis: "Food One-Worders" (6th Grade, Week 11: More Food), "One-Worders" (8th Grade, Week 26: Nonsense); copyright ©2013 by J. Patrick Lewis. Used with permission of Curtis Brown, Ltd. All rights reserved.

George Ella Lyon: "That Boat" (6th Grade, Week 32: Metaphor & Simile), "Saved by the Book" (7th Grade, Week 29: Poetry Poems), "How Romantic Can You Get?" (8th Grade, Week 21: Love & Friendship); copyright ©2013 by George Ella Lyon. Used with permission of the author. All rights reserved.

Guadalupe Garcia McCall: "The Café" (8th Grade, Week 13: Families), "The Boy" (8th Grade, Week 22: A Kinder Place); copyright ©2013 by Guadalupe Garcia McCall. Used with permission of the author. All rights reserved.

Heidi Mordhorst: "Meet The Saurus" (6th Grade, Week 28: Books); copyright ©2013 by Heidi Mordhorst. Used with permission of the author. All rights reserved.

Marilyn Nelson: "The Deaf Boy" (7th Grade, Week 25: Song & Dance), "Council of Brothers" (8th Grade, Week 23: Exploring); copyright ©2013 by Marilyn Nelson. Used with permission of the author. All rights reserved.

Lesléa Newman: "After the Blizzard, Outside My Window" (7th Grade, Week 9: Weather), "Mangoes" (7th Grade, Week 31: Different Forms), "According to Bread" (8th Grade, Week 32: Metaphor & Simile); copyright ©2013 by Lesléa Newman. Used with permission of the author. All rights reserved.

Naomi Shihab Nye: "Texas, Out Driving" (6th Grade, Week 34: On the Move), "For Bucky" (8th Grade, Week 4: Pets), "Editorial Suggestions" (8th Grade, Week 27: World of Words); copyright ©2013 by Naomi Shihab Nye. Used with permission of the author. All rights reserved.

Ann Whitford Paul: "Safe in My Shell" (8th Grade, Week 6: On the Ground); copyright ©2013 by Ann Whitford Paul. Used with permission of the author. All rights reserved.

Jack Prelutsky: "Dear Monster of Loch Ness" (6th Grade, Week 7: In the Water); copyright ©2013 by Jack Prelutsky. Used with permission of the author. All rights reserved.

Mary Quattlebaum: "What I Want to Be" (7th Grade, Week 10: Food), "Braces" (8th Grade, Week 11: More Food); copyright ©2013 by Mary Quattlebaum. Used with permission of the author. All rights reserved.

Heidi Bee Roemer: "Food Fest" (8th Grade, Week 10: Food); copyright ©2013 by Heidi Bee Roemer. Used with permission of the author. All rights reserved.

Michael J. Rosen: "Monday's Cat" (7th Grade, Week 5: More Pets), "Movies of Us" (8th Grade, Week 17: Time Together); copyright ©2013 by Michael J. Rosen. Used with permission of the author. All rights reserved.

Deborah Ruddell: "Sixth Grade Art Class" (6th Grade, Week 20: Art & Colors); copyright ©2013 by Deborah Ruddell. Used with permission of the author. All rights reserved.

Laura Purdie Salas: "Her Room" (8th Grade, Week 12: House & Home); copyright ©2013 by Laura Purdie Salas. Used with permission of the author. All rights reserved.

Michael Salinger: "Gear" (7th Grade, Week 24: Science & Technology), "Eviscerate" (8th Grade, Week 33: Personification); copyright ©2013 by Michael Salinger. Used with permission of the author. All rights reserved.

Ted Scheu: "I Know I'm Going Somewhere" (6th Grade, Week 36: Looking Forward); copyright ©2013 by Ted Scheu. Used with permission of the author. All rights reserved.

Joyce Sidman: "Convection" (6th Grade, Week 30: Rhyme, Repetition, & Rhythm), "Restless" (8th Grade, Week 34: On the Move); copyright ©2013 by Joyce Sidman. Used with permission of the author. All rights reserved.

Marilyn Singer: "Feather" (7th Grade, Week 6: On the Ground), "Body Art" (8th Grade, Week 35: Summer Vacation); copyright ©2013 by Marilyn Singer. Used with permission of the author. All rights reserved.

Ken Slesarik: "Season to Forgive" (7th Grade, Week 16: Holidays); copyright ©2013 by Ken Slesarik. Used with permission of the author. All rights reserved.

Sonya Sones: "Sitting for Trishie Devlin" (7th Grade, Week 14: Community); copyright ©2013 by Sonya Sones. Used with permission of the author. All rights reserved.

Eileen Spinelli: "Advice to Rapunzel" (6th Grade, Week 21: Love & Friendship); copyright ©2013 by Eileen Spinelli. Used with permission of the author. All rights reserved.

Holly Thompson: "Cod" (8th Grade, Week 36: Looking Forward); copyright ©2013 by Holly Thompson. Used with permission of the author. All rights reserved.

Amy Ludwig VanDerwater: "First Practice" (6th Grade, Week 14: Community), "Saying No" (7th Grade, Week 11: More Food); copyright ©2013 by Amy Ludwig VanDerwater. Used with permission of Curtis Brown, Ltd. All rights reserved.

Lee Wardlaw: "Cat Hockey" (6th Grade, Week 4: Pets); copyright ©2013 by Lee Wardlaw. Used with permission of Curtis Brown, Ltd. All rights reserved.

Charles Waters: "Fishing Trip" (6th Grade, Week 17: Time Together), "Cousins" (6th Grade, Week 35: Summer Vacation), "5 O'clock Shadow" (8th Grade, Week 18: Human Body); copyright ©2013 by Charles Waters. Used with permission of the author. All rights reserved.

April Halprin Wayland: "In the Word Woods" (6th Grade, Week 29: Poetry Poems), "I Had a Nightmare" (8th Grade, Week 19: More Human Body); copyright ©2013 by April Halprin Wayland. Used with permission of the author. All rights reserved.

Robert Weinstock: "Mere Shadow" (6th Grade, Week 26: Nonsense); copyright ©2013 by Robert Weinstock. Used with permission of the author. All rights reserved.

Steven Withrow: "Leafy Sea Dragon" (8th Grade, Week 7: In the Water); copyright ©2013 by Steven Withrow. Used with permission of the author. All rights reserved.

Allan Wolf: "Your Appendix Is a Mystery" (6th Grade, Week 18: Human Body); copyright ©2013 by Allan Wolf. Used with permission of the author. All rights reserved.

Virginia Euwer Wolff: "What She Asked" (7th Grade, Week 2: More School), "Doors of the 24-Hour Emergency Veterinary Hospital" (8th Grade, Week 5: More Pets); copyright ©2013 by Virginia Euwer Wolff. Used with permission of Curtis Brown, Ltd. All rights reserved.

Janet Wong: "First Week of School" (6th Grade, Week 1: School), "Wong's Café" (6th Grade, Week 16: Holidays), "Another New Year" (7th Grade, Week 1: School), "The Way You Might Judge" (8th Grade, Week 1: School), "Community Service" (8th Grade, Week 14: Community); copyright ©2013 by Janet Wong. Used with permission of the author. All rights reserved.

Jane Yolen: "Consider the Bombardier Beetle" (6th Grade, Week 6: On the Ground), "Giving" (6th Grade, Week 15: Stuff We Love), "Wilbur Asks Charlotte Ten Questions" (7th Grade, Week 28: Books); copyright ©2013 by Jane Yolen. Used with permission of Curtis Brown, Ltd. All rights reserved.

*"If I feel physically as if **the top of my head were taken off**, I know that is poetry."*

Emily Dickinson

TGIF!

We hope that you are finding Fridays even more special now that you're taking a few minutes each week to share a poem with your students on Poetry Friday. Spending time together with a funny, thoughtful, or interesting poem is a terrific way to develop a classroom community, talk about our feelings and experiences, and learn new words and concepts. And if you've shared 36 poems (one per week throughout the school year), we hope it has also become a beloved tradition.

Have you been marking this book up with notes about your favorite poems and strategies for sharing poetry? If not, go back and do that now. Add whatever you remember about students' responses to individual poems. We want this book to become one of the most useful resources in your professional library—as well as one of your favorite books for sharing aloud.

Wouldn't it be wonderful if this Poetry Friday experience was part of every grade level for every student? What a culture of literacy and language love that would create! **Please help us in spreading the word about the power of poetry** and ensuring that every child has a chance to experience these fabulous five minutes every Friday!

About this Book

"In looking at some apparently small object, **one feels the swirl of great events***.*"

— William Carlos Williams

Acknowledgments

Janet likes to call us "poetry evangelists." At the same time, though, she sometimes wonders if we are preaching to the choir about the glory of poetry.

This book represents an effort to reach beyond the choir—to preach poetry on the street corner. We hope that this book inspires teachers who are new to poetry or haven't read much poetry in years. If you liked this book, please tell the world—or at least your colleagues in your school and school district. If any of your fellow teachers are not in the habit of sharing poetry, those are the people we need you to talk to first!

The different editions of *The Poetry Friday Anthology* (for K–5 and 6–8 in paperback and also e-book formats for the Common Core and the TEKS) represent our efforts to achieve "Poetry Plus"—facilitating the teaching of poetry through easy-to-do, step-by-step curriculum suggestions for hundreds of original poems.

We cannot praise enough the generosity of the community of poets who write for young people. This is an extraordinary group and we continue to be humbled by their willingness to participate in our projects. The poets who contributed to our *PoetryTagTime* trio of digital anthologies and to *The Poetry Friday Anthology* are the best in our field. Please get to know them and their books on their individual pages in the Meet the Poets sections at our website.

A final note: our sincere thanks to our readers and book buyers and book sharers and Poetry Friday Ambassadors for their support. Please visit our blogs and continue to spread the word about our books!

With deepest appreciation,

Sylvia and Janet

www.PomeloBooks.com
www.PoetryTagTime.com
PFAMS.Blogspot.com
PoetryFridayAnthology.Blogspot.com

About Sylvia Vardell

Sylvia M. Vardell is Professor in the School of Library and Information Studies at Texas Woman's University and has taught graduate courses in children's and young adult literature at various universities since 1981. Vardell has published extensively, including five books on literature for children, as well as over twenty book chapters and one hundred journal articles. Her current work focuses on poetry for children, including a regular blog, *PoetryforChildren,* since 2006. She is also the regular "Everyday Poetry" columnist for ALA's *Book Links* magazine.

Vardell has served as a member or chair of several national award committees including the NCTE Award for Poetry, the NCTE Notables, the Cybils Poetry Award, the ALA Odyssey Award for audiobooks, the ALA Sibert Award for informational literature, and the NCTE Orbis Pictus Award for nonfiction, among others. She has conducted over one hundred presentations at state, regional, national, and international conferences, and has received grants from the Young Adult Library Service Association (YALSA), Ezra Jack Keats Foundation, National Council of Teachers of English (NCTE), the Assembly on Literature for Young Adults Foundation, the Texas Library Association, and the National Endowment for the Humanities. She taught at the University of Zimbabwe in Africa as a Fulbright scholar and is a consultant to the Poetry Foundation.

Other Professional Books by Sylvia Vardell

Poetry Aloud Here: Sharing Poetry with Children (2012)
The Poetry Teacher's Book of Lists (2012)
Children's Literature in Action: A Librarian's Guide (2008)
Poetry People: A Practical Guide to Children's Poets (2007)
Literature-based Instruction with English Language Learners (2002; with Nancy Hadaway and Terrell Young)

About Janet Wong

Janet S. Wong is a graduate of Yale Law School and former lawyer who switched careers and became a children's poet. Her dramatic career change has been featured on *The Oprah Winfrey Show*, CNN's *Paula Zahn Show*, and *Radical Sabbatical*. She is the author of thirty books for children and teens on a wide variety of subjects, including writing and revision (*You Have to Write*), creative recycling (*The Dumpster Diver*), diversity and community (*Apple Pie 4th of July*), cheating on tests (*Me and Rolly Maloo*), and chess (*Alex and the Wednesday Chess Club*).

Wong has served as a member of several national committees including the NCTE Award for Poetry, the NCTE Commission on Literature, the Notable Books for a Global Society committee of the International Reading Association (IRA), the SCBWI Golden Kite committee (for picture books), and the PEN Center USA Literary Award committee (for children's literature). Wong is a frequent featured or keynote speaker at conferences and has worked with over 200,000 children at schools all over the world. Her recent focus is the exploration of digital opportunities for children's books; she encourages children not just to read e-books, but also to publish their own writing using affordable new technologies.

Selected Poetry Books by Janet Wong

Declaration of Interdependence: Poems for an Election Year (2012)
Once Upon a Tiger: New Beginnings for Endangered Animals (2011)
TWIST: Yoga Poems (2007)
Knock on Wood: Poems about Superstitions (2003)
Behind the Wheel: Poems about Driving (1999)
The Rainbow Hand: Poems about Mothers and Children (1999)
A Suitcase of Seaweed (1996)
Good Luck Gold (1994)

Praise for
The Poetry Friday Anthology K-5 Edition

"Be careful when reading this highly-addictive anthology. . . . **Find a place for this book on your desk** since you'll be turning to it time and time again. You may even want two copies, one for your students and one for your own use."

—Barbara Ward
Washington State University Pullman
from a review in IRA's *Reading Today*

"In addition to the poetry, Vardell and Wong offer *Take 5!* ideas that focus on reading each poem aloud and talking about the poem, with follow-up guidelines for oral and choral reading of more poetry . . . **This is a lot of resource and professional development** for $29.99!"

—Jeanette Larson, from The ALSC Blog

"**It's a *vade mecum* for the elementary teacher** and a word magnet for the K-5 child. Brava to the anthologists and the poets!"

—J. Patrick Lewis, Children's Poet Laureate

"The Common Core standards provided throughout the book **give teachers confidence that they are integrating key skills** as they share the poems. The book highlights and documents specific skills and techniques, such as rhyme, repetition, rhythm, and alliteration, as they are used one poem at a time."

—U.S. Kids Magazine (Parents & Teachers)

**Look for the PoetryTagTime e-book series:
PoetryTagTime, P*TAG (for teens), and Gift Tag!**

pomelo * books

p*tag is the first electronic-only poetry anthology for teens

31 poems and prose pieces inspired by photos

one poem connects to another by sharing three words . . .

students can play along at The P*TAG Blog: TeenPoetryTagTime.Blogspot.com

pick a photo and write about it
in prose
then in a poem
then tag another student
to do the same

after everyone is done
project the e-book on a screen
and see what the P*TAG poets did
with the same photos

P*TAG poets, in order of appearance:

Marilyn Singer	David L. Harrison	Jen Bryant
Betsy Franco	Lorie Ann Grover	Kathi Appelt
Allan Wolf	Julie Larios	Helen Frost
Naomi Shihab Nye	Michele Krueger	J. Patrick Lewis
Sara Holbrook	April Halprin Wayland	JonArno Lawson
Charles Waters	Stephanie Hemphill	Sonya Sones
Michael Salinger	Heidi Mordhorst	Lee Bennett Hopkins
Joyce Sidman	Tracie Vaughn Zimmer	Jaime Adoff
Margarita Engle	Paul B. Janeczko	Janet Wong
Jeannine Atkins	Arnold Adoff	
Steven Withrow	Kimberly Marcus	with photos by Sylvia Vardell

Made in the USA
Charleston, SC
29 June 2013